This book is dedicated to my mother, Ethel Shimizu, who is the best mother and friend—and the best "photographer."

Mahalo
to Jodi Fukumoto for graciously sharing her owl and plumeria origami designs from her book **The Guide to Hawaiian-Style Money Folds,** *and to*

Mom & Dad

Elaine Mezurashi

Yuki & Audrey Toguchi

Photo Trends, Pearlridge

Sweet Laurente-Nunez

Mutual Publishing

Mardee Melton

And most of all, my great family:

Karl, Karley, and Kamren

Table of Contents

MONEY
Lei Making
IN HAWAI'I
A STEP-BY-STEP GUIDE

2

Laurie Shimizu Ide

MUTUAL PUBLISHING

Library of Congress Cataloging-in-Publica-
tion Data

Ide, Laurie Shimizu.
  Money lei making in Hawaii 2 : a step-by-
step guide / by Laurie Shimizu Ide.
      p. cm.
  Includes bibliographical references and
index.
  ISBN 1-56647-867-7 (softcover : alk. paper)
1. Origami. 2. Leis--Hawaii. 3. Paper money--
United States. I. Title.
TT870.I34 2008
736'.982--dc22

                                    2008004606
First Printing, May 2008

Book design by Mardee Melton

ISBN-10: 1-56647-867-7
ISBN-13: 978-1-56647-867-0

Mutual Publishing, LLC
1215 Center Street, Suite 210
Honolulu, Hawai'i 96816
Ph: (808) 732-1709
Fax: (808) 734-4094
Email: info@mutualpublishing.com
www.mutualpublishing.com

Printed in Korea

How cool is *a money lei?*
TOTALLY COOL!

A money lei is always appreciated, cherished, and loved by everyone.

Introduction

A MONEY LEI is always appreciated, cherished, and loved. It is always the best and most memorable lei compared to any floral lei. The best thing is that a money lei has value after it is used. It has life after the occasion–spending life.

Money lei making is a combination of giving a monetary gift and a lei of love. A money lei may be made with bills and/or coins.

In this book, I have combined the Japanese culture of origami and money gift giving with the Hawaiian culture of lei making. Dollar bills folded origami-style and made into a lei puts a contemporary, cultural twist on the traditional lei.

In Hawai'i, a lei is given on birthdays, graduations, weddings, retirements, and all other events celebrating many important occasions. A money lei is given on birthdays using the dollar amount of the person's age. It is often given at retirement parties using the amount of years in dollars. But most of all, a money lei is very popular in Hawai'i during the graduation season, using school color ribbons.

Money folding is a form of origami. Japanese origami literally means "to fold paper." If you are new to origami or money folding, I welcome you to this book of easy-to-follow folding directions. You do not need to know what the complex symbols and arrows mean that are in other origami folding books. This book shows the actual bill in each step, making the directions easy to follow. Consider your first bill

folded as your practice piece. The practice piece may have unnecessary creases; therefore a used bill is okay. Usually the second and third attempts will turn out better. For best folding results, use a new, crisp bill. Line up all edges and corners as precisely as possible. Fold on a hard, flat surface. Good lighting is a must. If you cannot get new bills, iron clean, nice bills to smooth and remove the wrinkles and moisture of used bills. Use medium heat.

I also use a lot of purchased embellishments such as stickers, confetti, parts of a fountain centerpiece, computer clipart, and pre-made laser-cut designs, making it easier and faster to create a lei. You may also use large paper punch-outs to create your own scrapbook-like embellishments. Many clipart ideas may be found at **www.free-clipart-pictures.net**. Pre-made laser-cut designs shown in this book may be found at **www.hulahlahs.com**.

There are many exciting ways to fold bills to create a unique money lei. This book shows thirty-one money lei projects. Feel free to mix and match the ideas to create your own unique lei. This book will ignite your creative imagination for your own new money lei ideas.

All U.S. currency is government property. It is legal to fold and tape bills, but illegal to intentionally destroy money by gluing, cutting, or tearing it in any manner.

Use the least amount of tape as possible.

When taking apart a money lei, SLOWLY and GENTLY remove the double-sided tape. Rub off the tape to prevent damage to the bill.

Bow-Tie Dollar Graduation Lei

One bill makes one bow tie. May substitute stickers for computer prints on card stock or party fountain centerpiece cutouts.

Makes a 47" lei.

MATERIALS:

- 11 dollar bills, crisp
- 8 nickels
- 2 yds. tape, double-sided 3/16"
- 15 graduation stickers or similar
- 1 graduation pendant/ medallion or similar
- 1 ft. plastic wrap
- 2 yds. button thread, white
- 1 scissors

1. Fold the bill in half lengthwise. Open the fold.

2. Fold the two sides of the bill inward toward the center fold.

3. Fold the bill in half lengthwise. Open the fold.

4. Fold the bill in half widthwise.

5. Fold the two creased corners of the bill downward evenly, forming a point. Open the fold.

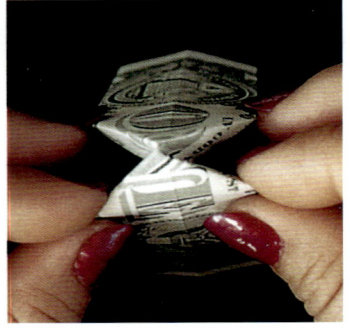

6. Push in the two sides of the bill at the crease, forming a point.

7. Fold the two sides of the bill upward and crease.

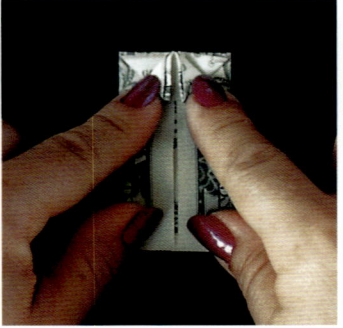

8. Fold the two corners on the top layer of the bill downward evenly, forming a point. Flip the bill.

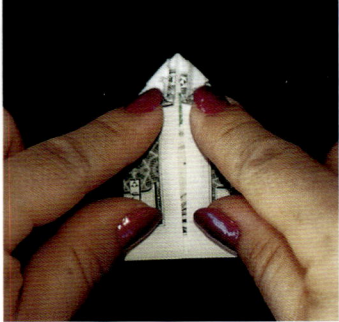

9. Fold the two top corners of the bill downward evenly, forming a point.

10. Pinch and pull the ends of the bill, holding down the triangle folds with your thumbs. Stop pulling when the bottom centerfold of the bill lifts up. Push down and flatten the center of the bill.

11. Tape down the back center of the bill to secure the bow tie using double-sided tape.

12. Fold the four corners of the bill inward, creating points. Open the folds.

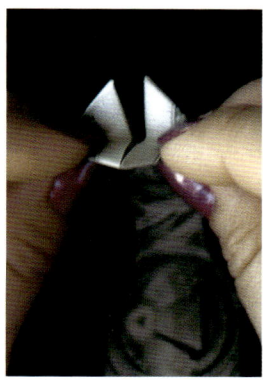  

13. Push in the two sides of the bill at the crease to form points. Repeat for the other side of the bill.

14. Tape the bow-tie bills together using double-sided tape. Tape on the top and bottom of the bills. Insert another bill. Press down to secure the bills. Continue until all bills are joined.

  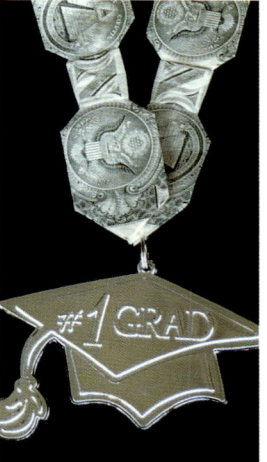

15. Wrap eight nickels with a small 2" x 2" square plastic wrap, tying the top with an 8" piece of thread. Cut off the excess plastic wrap.

16. Attach string to the medallion. Tape the medallion to one end of the lei using double-sided tape. Use a lot of tape to secure the medallion.

17. Tape the ends of the lei together using lots of double-sided tape.

18. Add the stickers and the nickels evenly around the lei using double-sided tape.

Butterfly Dollar Lei

One bill makes one butterfly. The nylon flowers shown may be purchased by the yard at your local giant retail chain store.

Makes a 70" lei.

MATERIALS:

10 dollar bills, crisp

12 flowers, nylon or similar

3 yds. tape, double-sided, 3/16"

2 ft. tape, double-sided, 3/4"

2 yds. ribbon, acetate, #9 (1-1/2"), purple

2 yds. ribbon, acetate, #5 (7/8"), lavender

1 glue gun and 3 glue sticks

3 yds. thread, button/carpet, purple

1 sewing needle

1 tape measure

1 scissors

1. Fold the bill in half widthwise.

2. Fold the bill in half lengthwise.

3. Place your right pointer in the top opening of the bill. Push up toward the inside corner. Push the folded edge down flattening it, forming a triangle point. Flip the bill.

4. Place your left pointer in the opening of the bill. Push up toward the inside corner. Push the folded edge down flattening it, forming a triangle point. Turn the bill.

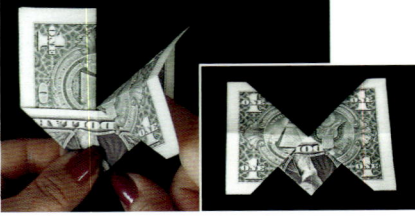

5. Place your right pointer in the right opening of the bill. Bend the bill downward, overlapping the top of the triangle. Push the crease of the bill down until it is flat, forming the triangle wing. Repeat this step for the left side of the bill, forming the left wing.

6. Pinch and tuck in the middle of the wing on both sides of the bill.

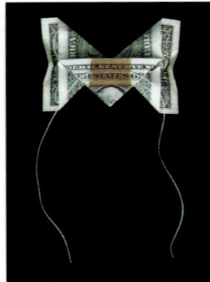

7. Cut a piece of thread 10" in length. Place a 1" piece of the 3/4" double-sided tape to the back of the butterfly. Stick on the thread in the center of the tape. Place another 1" piece of the 3/4" double-sided tape over the thread to secure it. White thread is used for these photos.

8. Pull down both sides of the wings. Tape the wings to the body of the butterfly, using double-sided tape.

9. Cut a strip of purple and lavender ribbon 70" in length. Place a long strip of double-sided tape along the back of the lavender ribbon. Remove the paper backing while sticking the lavender ribbon to the center of the purple ribbon. Cut the ends of the ribbon to a "w" tip. Position the butterfly bills and flowers evenly along both sides of the ribbon. Start about 4" from each end of the ribbon.

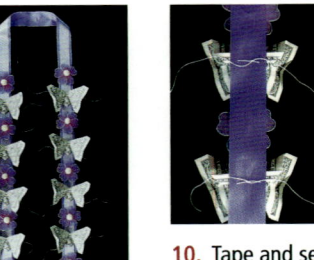

10. Tape and sew the butterflies to the ribbon. Tie a knot in the back of the ribbon.

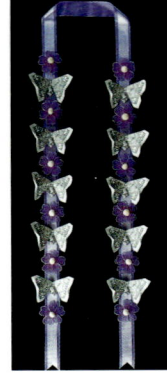

11. Glue the flowers to the ribbon using hot glue.

Chain Dollar Lei

One bill makes one chain link. This lei can be made in less than an hour.

$28.00 makes a 40" lei.

MATERIALS:

28 dollar bills, crisp

2-1/2 yds. tape, double-sided, 3/16"

1 scissors

1. Fold the two edges of the bill inward about a fourth from the top and bottom, centering George Washington's picture.

2. Flatten the creases using a pen.

3. Tape one end of the back of each bill using double-sided tape. Repeat steps 1 to 3 for all bills.

4. Peel off the paper backing of the tape for one bill. Bend and tape the bill into a loop.

5. Insert another bill into the loop of the first bill. Peel off the paper backing of the tape. Bend and tape the bill into a loop. Position the bills to face the same pattern. Continue until all bills are joined.

6. Connect the first and last bills to join the lei.

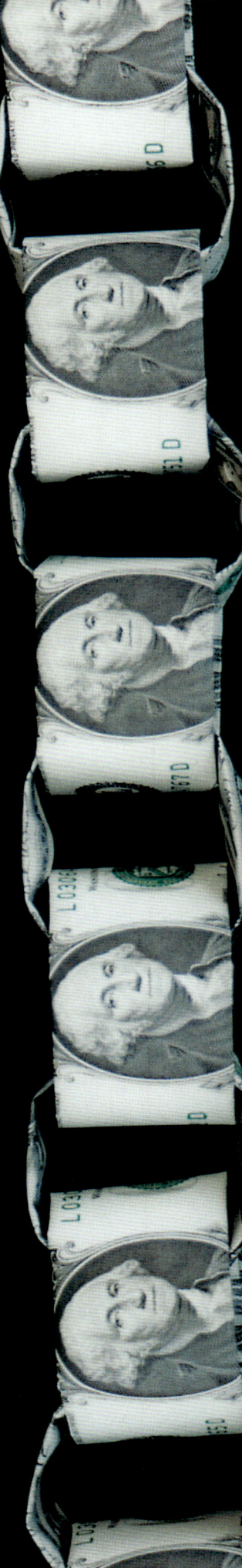

Crane "Long Life" Dollar Lei

*Two bills make one crane. Fold the corners perfectly to keep the points neat. It's a great lei for a retirement or birthday party. Visit **www.hulahlahs.com** for the crane and "long life" laser-cut prints.*

Makes a 70" lei.

MATERIALS:

12 dollar bills, crisp

6 silver dollars or Las Vegas $1.00 tokens

1 roll tape, double-sided, 3/16"

2 yds. tape, transparent, 1/2" or similar

6 yds. ribbon, acetate, #16 (2-1/4"), red

6 origami sheets, 3" x 3", gold

1 pkgs. "Long Life" Asian laser cutouts, or similar

2 pkgs. crane Asian laser cutouts, or similar (6 cranes)

2 yds. thread, button/carpet, red

1 sewing needle

1 tape measure

1 scissors

1. Place double-sided tape along the bottom edge of the bill. Stick another bill onto the taped bill.

2. Fold the left side of the bill inward leaving 1-1/16" uncovered.

3. Fold the two corners of the bill upward forming a point. Open the folds.

4. Push in the two sides of the bill downward to the crease, forming an even point. Turn the bill.

5. Fold the right and left tip of the top layer of the bill upward to the center crease. Open these two last folds.

6. Push in the right-top side of the bill at the crease, forming an even point at the top. Repeat for the left-top side of the bill.

7. Pull the center-front opening of the bill downward. Crease the two top tips of the bill evenly. Flatten the formed diamond-shape.

8. Fold the two bottom edges of the bill inward forming two narrow tips. Open these two last folds.

9. Push in the two sides of the bill at the crease to tuck the backside in. Flip the bill.

10. Fold the top of the bill downward 1-1/16". Fold the bottom of the bill upward, bending it slightly over the top flap. Flip the bill.

11. Open and bend the left-top point of the bill down 1/2" to form the head of the crane.

12. Wrap a silver dollar coin with gold origami paper.

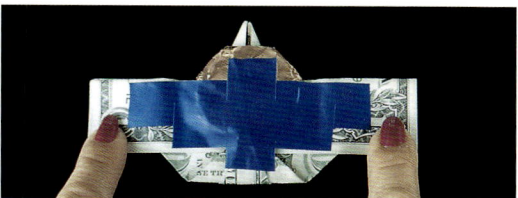

13. Tape the coin to the bill about 3/4" above the folded edge to secure the coin. Tape down the bottom flap of the bill over the coin for added security. Blue tape is used for this photo.

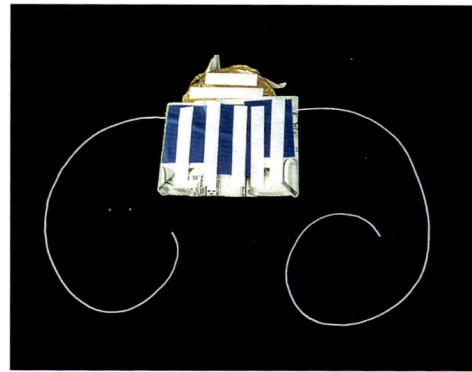

14. Fold the two sides of the bill inward. Tape the ends of the bill down with tape. Tape a 12" length of red thread to the back of the bill. Add double-sided tape generously to adhere the bill to the ribbon. Blue tape and white thread are used for this photo.

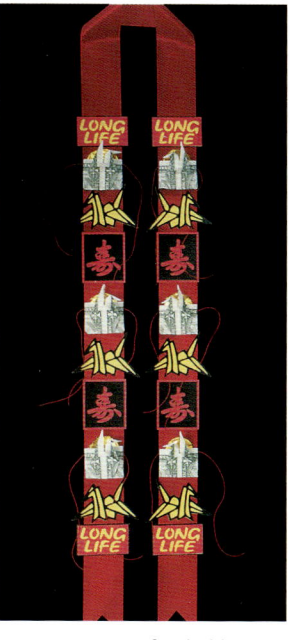

15. Cut a strip of red ribbon 70" in length. Cut the edges of the ribbon to a "w" tip. Position the cranes and stickers/cut-outs evenly on both sides of the ribbon.

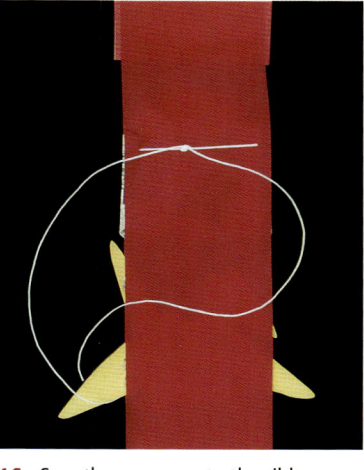

16. Sew the cranes onto the ribbon using a sewing needle. Knot the thread in the back of the ribbon. White thread is used for this photo.

13

Daisy Dollar Lei

Three bills make one daisy. For a greenish flower use the back of the dollar bill. Place glue in the hole where you cut the stem off the silk flower using the tip of a wire. Glue helps to keep the flower petal layers together.

Makes a 70" lei.

MATERIALS:

24 dollar bills, crisp

1 stem silk daisy flowers, or similar, yellow (8 blooms)

2 yds. ribbon, acetate, #9 (1-1/2"), white

2 yds. ribbon, acetate, #5 (7/8"), yellow

3 yds. tape, double-sided, 3/16"

12 butterflies, nylon, 1", yellow

4 florist wires, #26 or similar

3 yds. thread, carpet/button, white

1 sewing needle

1 hot glue gun and 3 glue sticks

1 wire cutter

1 pen

1 tape measure

1 scissors

1. Fold the bill in half widthwise to form a crease. Open the bill.

2. Fold the two sides of the bill inward toward the center crease.

3. Fold the bill in half lengthwise.

4. Fold the four corners of the bill inward to the center crease.

5. Fold the top and bottom sides of the bill inward to the center crease.

6. Fold the bill into fourths lengthwise in an accordion-pleated pattern. Repeat steps 1 to 6 for two additional bills.

7. Fold the three bills in half widthwise to form a crease.

8. Cut a piece of wire into thirds. Tie the wire around the center of the three folded bills. Place the center bill facing the opposite direction. Twist the wire tight, securing the three bills.

9. Open the petals using the back of a pen.

10. Cut off the excess wire using a wire cutter. Use the back of a pen to flatten down the wire against the flower. Tie a 10" thread around the wire. Leave the thread long. Add double-sided tape to the back of the flowers. Place the tape over the thread.

11. Cut pieces of white and yellow ribbon 70" in length. Tape the yellow ribbon to the center of the white ribbon using a 70" strip of double-sided tape. Cut the ends to a "w" tip. Position the four money flowers, four silk daisies, and five butterflies evenly on each side of the ribbon. Start 3" from the ends of the ribbon.

12. Peel off the paper backing of the tape. Stick and sew the money flowers to the ribbon using a sewing needle. Glue the silk daisies and butterflies onto the ribbon.

Diamond Dollar Lei

One bill makes three diamonds. This lei is fast and easy to make. Must use strong double-sided tape. May add decorations to the lei.

Makes a 50" lei.

MATERIALS:

20 dollar bills, crisp
1 roll tape, double-sided, strong, 3/16"
1 scissors

1. Place the back of the bill facing up. Fold the four corners of the bill inward toward the center.

2. Fold the top and bottom of the bill inward about 9/16".

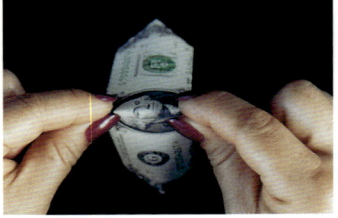

3. Bend the bill in half widthwise. Make a small crease at the top and bottom of the center of the bill. Do not crease the face of the bill.

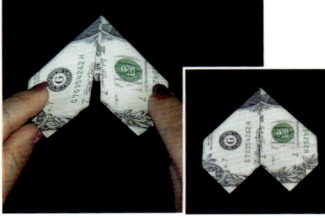

4. Fold the two sides of the bill downward toward the center of the bill to form a crease. Open the fold.

5. Turn the bill around. Fold the two sides of the bill downward toward the center of the bill to form a crease. Open the fold.

6. Push in the two sides of the bill, bending it at the previously formed creases.

7. Rotate the bill. Repeat step 6 for the other side of the bill, pushing in at the previously formed creases.

8. Place the bill facing down. Fold the two ends outward. Press the two end flat.

9. Fold in the four middle corners of the bill, forming two inside points.

10. Place double-sided tape under the folds to secure the fold.

11. Place a small piece of strong double-sided tape on the end of one diamond of the folded bill. Stick on another bill to form the lei. Continue until all bills are taped together.

12. Overlap and join the two ends of the lei together using a large piece of double-sided tape.

Diploma Dollar Graduation Duck Lei

One bill makes one diploma. Be careful when piercing the ducks.

Makes a 38" lei.

MATERIALS:

- 9 dollar bills, crisp
- 1-1/4 yds. double-sided tape, 3/16" or transparent tape
- 3 yds. ribbon, acetate, #1 (1/4"), black
- 1 needle, yarn, tapestry, or similar
- 3 yds. lei twine or crochet thread, white
- 1 toothpick
- 8 rubber ducks
- 1 tape measure
- 1 scissors

1. Place double-sided tape along the right edge of the bill.

2. Roll the bill widthwise, forming a 1/4" tube. Peel off the paper backing of the tape. Stick the end of the bill down to secure the tube.

3. Place double-sided tape around the center of the rolled bill. Peel off the paper backing of the tape.

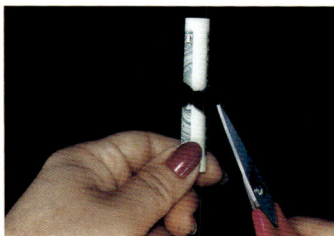

4. Cut a 6" strip of ribbon. Tie a bow around the rolled bill to create the diploma. Trim off the excess ribbon. Repeat steps 1 to 4 for all nine bills.

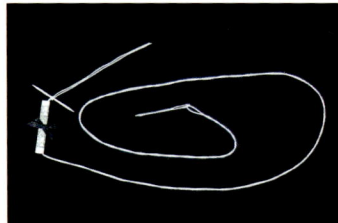

5. Cut a piece of thread 104" in length. Thread the needle. Tie a knot 6" from the open end of the thread. Tie a toothpick in the knot to secure the first bill. Add the first bill to the string upside down. Pull the bill down to the end of the string.

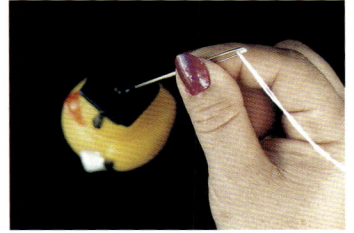

6. Pierce a rubber duck from the top through the bottom. Pull the duck down to the end of the string. Continue stringing on four additional bills upside-down and three ducks in an alternating pattern.

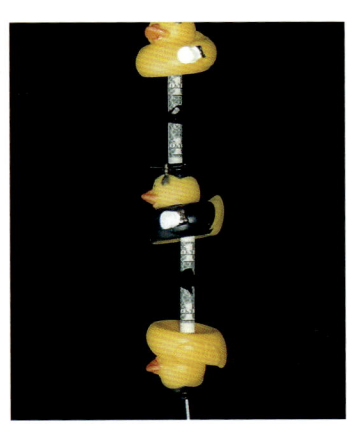

7. String on the fifth duck upside-down. Pierce from the bottom of the rubber duck through the top.

8. String on four additional bills right side up and the three remaining ducks, piercing from the bottom through the top in an alternating pattern. Tie a knot to close the lei. Add a bow if desired.

Double Carnation Dollar Lei

One bill makes one floweret. To cut cost, substitute decorated or solid color paper for bills or add straw between bills.

Makes a 40" lei with 1/8" folds. $80.00 will make a 40" lei with 1/4" folds.

MATERIALS:

120 dollar bills, crisp

18 yds. button thread, white

1 roll tape, double-sided 3/16"

1 sewing needle, 2" or longer

1 tape measure

1 scissors

1 toothpick

1. Fold the bill into 1/2" folds, creating an accordion pattern.

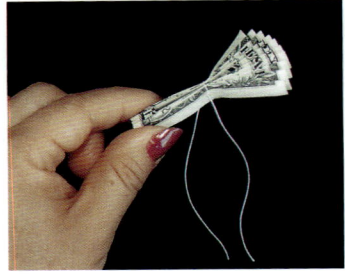

2. Tie a knot in the center of the bill to secure it. Use a piece of thread 6" in length. Trim off the excess string.

3. Place double-sided tape along both ends of the bill covering the knot. Cut the tape at the end of the bill.

4. Peel off the paper backing of the tape. Stick the tape ends together creating a circular disk. Repeat steps 1 to 4 until all bills are circular.

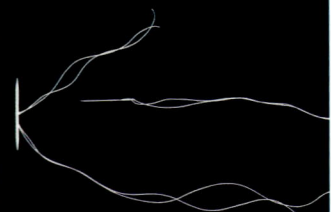

5. Cut a piece of thread 112" in length. Thread the needle. Fold the thread in half. Tie a knot 6" from the open end of the thread. Tie a toothpick in the knot to secure the first bill.

6. String on the bills by inserting the needle through the loop on the tied bill, then out through the space between the taped edges. Be careful not to pierce the bill.

7. Repeat until all bills are strung. Tie a square knot to join the lei. Add a bow if desired.

Fan Dollar "Long Life" Lei

Two bills make one set of fans. Use a 75" ribbon for a taller recipient. Space the items evenly. This is a popular lei for a "Yakudoshi" or "Kanreki" special milestone birthday party. The Japanese symbol on the paper fan means long life and happiness.

Makes a 70" lei.

MATERIALS:

20 dollar bills, crisp

8 fan picks, 2.5", "Senjyu" red paper or similar

2 yds. ribbon, acetate, #16 (2-1/4"), red

5 yds. ribbon, acetate, #1H (3/8"), red

5 yds. ribbon, metallic, 1/8", gold

1 yd. tape, double-sided, 3/4"

10 silk flowers, mini, gold

10 florist wires, #24

1 roll floral tape, 1/2", dark green

1 glue gun and 3 to 4 glue sticks

3 yds. thread, button/carpet, red

1 sewing needle

1 wire cutter

1 pen or pencil

1 tape measure

1 scissors

1. Fold the bill into 1/8" folds, creating an accordion pattern. Fold all bills. Repeat this step for all bills.

2. Twist and fold the bill a third of the way upward to the left for five bills, creating a two-fan look with the smaller fan in the front of the larger fan. Twist and fold the bill upward a third of the way to the right for the remaining five bills.

3. Hook a 9" wire through the bent crease of the double fan. Wrap the wire two to three times around the base of the bill. Create a stem with the remaining wire.

4. Stretch and wrap floral tape around the wired part of the fan down to the end of the wire for all ten double fans.

5. Fold the base of the bill upward, creating a hook for the ten large fans.

6. Hook a half-length wire through the bent crease of the large fan. Wrap a 9" wire two to three times around the fan. Create a stem with the remaining wire. Stretch and wrap floral tape around the wired part of the fan down to the end of the wire as in steps 3 to 4. Repeat for a total of ten large fans.

7. Stretch and wrap the floral tape around the large and double fan to secure them together. Tape around the wired part of the fans down to the end of the wires.

8. Cut the wire stem to about 2" using a wire cutter. Curl the end of the wire using a pen or pencil.

9. Cut two strips of gold 1/8" ribbon 9" and 14" in length. Start a red bow by pinching 1" from the back end of the ribbon. Make a 1" forward loop on the top. Pinch them together.

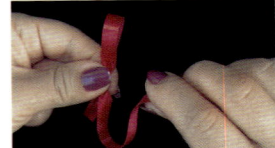

10. Twist the ribbon 180 degrees to the left, facing the back of the ribbon upward. Make a 1" forward loop on the bottom. Pinch them together to form the second loop.

11. Twist the ribbon 180 degrees to the right, facing the back of the ribbon on the top. Make a 1" forward loop on the top to form the third loop. Pinch them together. Repeat the loop-making steps 9 to 11 until six loops are formed, three on each side. Trim off the excess ribbon.

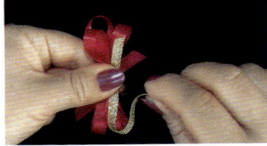

12. Add a 14" gold ribbon to the red bow by pinching 1" from the end of the ribbon. Make an upward loop about 1". Pinch the ribbons together. Continue steps 9 to 11, creating four loops, two on each side to make a double color bow.

13. Tie a knot where the ribbon is pinched using 9" strip of gold ribbon. Pull on the loops to fluff and even them out. Repeat steps 9 to 13 for a total of ten bows.

14. Tie the bows onto the ten fan clusters. Trim off the excess ribbon.

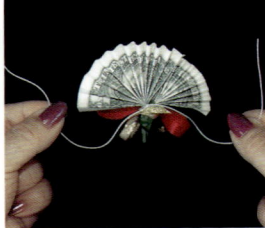

15. Tie a 10" length of thread around the taped stem of the fan. White thread was used for this photo.

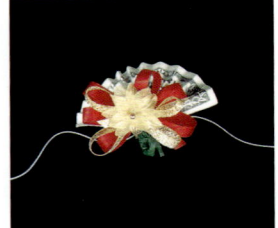

16. Glue a gold flower onto the center of the ribbon using hot glue. White thread was used for this photo.

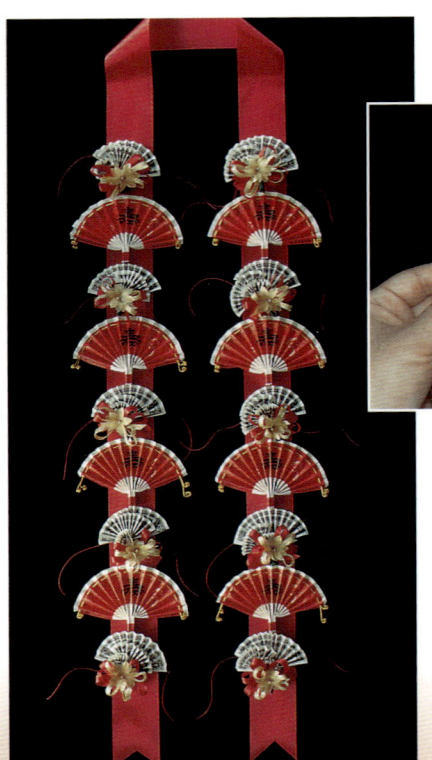

17. Cut a strip of ribbon 70" in length. Cut the two ends of the ribbon to a "w" tip. Bend the ribbon in half. Position the money fans and paper fans onto the ribbon spaced evenly. Start the lowest fan 4" from the bottom of the lei. Inset photo shows the removal of the fan pick.

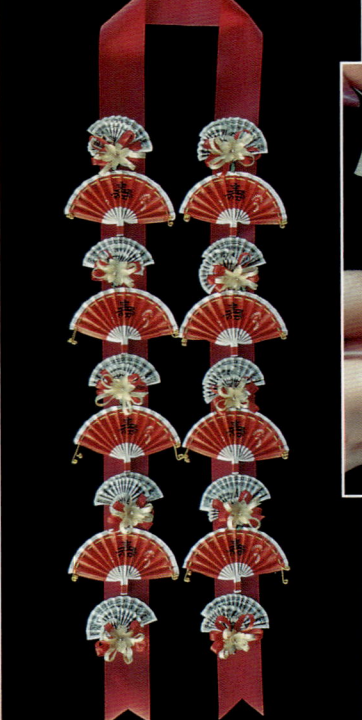

18. Glue the paper fans onto the ribbon. Sew the money fans to the ribbon using a sewing needle. White thread is used for this photo.

Felt Flower Penny Lei

Two pennies make one flower. Great for pre-school graduations and birthdays.

Makes a 40" lei.

MATERIALS:

- 34 pennies, shiny
- 1 sheet felt, thin, light pink
- 1 sheet felt, thin, dark pink
- 2 yds. ribbon, raffia, dark pink
- 1 glue gun and 3 glue sticks
- 2 ft. clear plastic wrap
- 3 yds. thread, button/carpet, white
- 1 sheet, cardstock, 6"
- 1 needle, yarn, tapestry or similar
- 1 tape measure
- 1 scissors

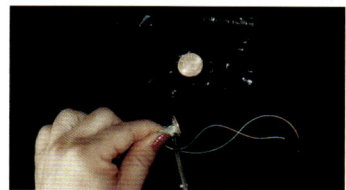

1. Cut a piece of plastic wrap into a 3" x 3" square. Wrap the penny in the center of the plastic wrap, head facing down. Twist the plastic wrap to tighten the slack. Tie a knot with thread to secure the penny. Trim off the excess thread and plastic wrap. Repeat this step for all pennies.

2. Make a flower-shape pattern on cardstock. Trace and cut out eight light-pink felt flowers and nine dark pink felt flowers using the pattern.

3. Cut two snips in the middle of each flower.

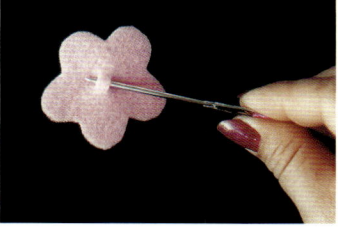

4. Cut a strip of raffia ribbon 60" in length. String on a dark pink felt flower using a needle. Pierce the flowers through the slits. Pull the blossom down to 10" from the end of the ribbon.

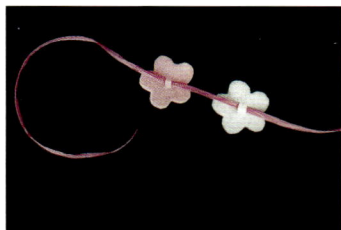

5. String a light pink flower onto the ribbon. Stop 1" from the end of the first flower. Continue stringing on all of the flowers in an alternating color pattern, stopping 1" from each flower.

6. Glue the covered pennies on both sides of the center of the flowers. Glue half of the pennies onto the flowers with the top of the heads facing the right end of the lei. Glue the other half of the pennies onto the flowers with the top of the heads facing the left end of the lei.

7. Tie a knot on each end of the raffia ribbon to prevent fraying. Tie a bow to close the lei.

Floweret Dollar Kukui Nut Lei

One bill makes one floweret. May substitute button/carpet thread for rubber bands.

Makes a 40" lei.

MATERIALS:

22 dollar bills, crisp

22 kukui nuts, black

44 cowry shell rings

1-1/2 yds. tape, double-sided, 3/16"

1 sewing needle

3 yds. thread, button/carpet, white

1 toothpick

1 scissors

1. Fold the bill widthwise into 1/8" folds, creating an accordion pattern.

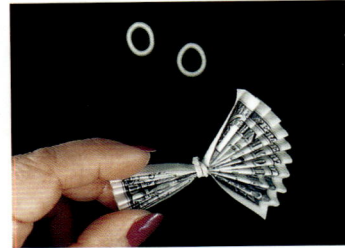

2. Place a rubber band in the center of the bill to secure the folds. Wrap the rubber band twice over the bill if needed.

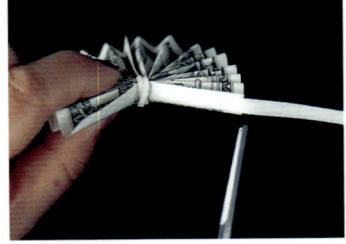

3. Place double-sided tape along the two sides of the folded bill. Peel off the paper backing.

4. Stick the ends of the bill together, forming a circle.

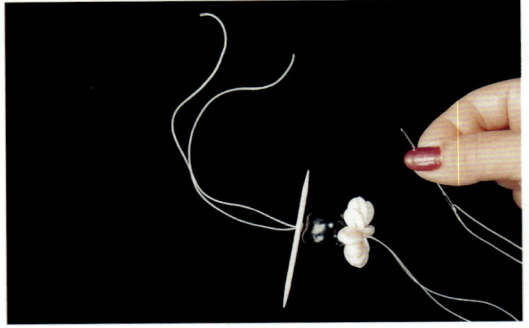

5. Cut a piece of thread 104" in length. Thread the needle. Fold the thread in half. Tie a knot 6" from the open end of the thread. Attach a toothpick to the knotted end to secure the first kukui nut. String through one kukui nut and one shell ringlet.

6. Insert the needle through the rubber band loop, then out through the space between the taped edges of the bill. Pull the bill down to the last shell ringlet.

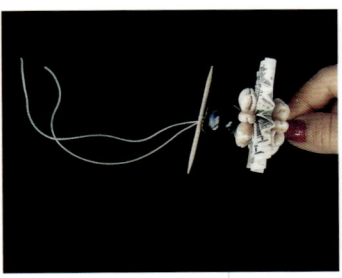

7. String on one ringlet to secure the bill. Repeat steps 1 to 7 until lei is completed.

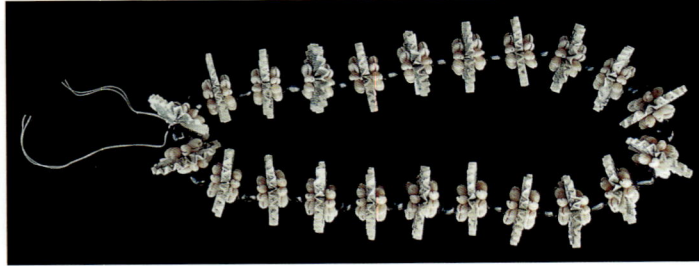

8. Tie a knot to join and secure the lei. Add a bow if desired.

Fortune Cookie Dollar Good Luck Lei

Two bills make one fortune cookie. The Chinese "Happiness" symbols are from confetti or may be taken from a fountain centerpiece. Visit **www.hulahlahs.com** *for the fortune cookie laser-cut prints.*

Makes a 70" lei.

MATERIALS:

- 20 dollar bills, crisp
- 6 fortune cookie stickers or similar (scrap book cutouts or computer clipart on card stock paper)
- 12 Chinese "Happiness/ Blessing & Good Wishes" symbols or similar
- 2 yds. ribbon, acetate, #16, (2-1/4"), red
- 3 yds. ribbon, metallic, #9, (1-1/2"), gold
- 6 yds. thread, button, red
- 1 sewing needle
- 1 roll double-sided tape, 3/16"
- 10 "Good Luck" fortune cookie computer tags on white paper, 3-1/2" x 1/2"
- 1 tape measure

1. Tape along the bottom front of the bill using double-sided tape.

2. Stick a second bill along the taped edge.

3. Fold the two sides of the bill inward about 1".

4. Fold the bottom-right and top-left corner of the bill inward, slightly over the folded flap.

5. Overlap the top of the bill over the bottom of the bill diagonally, about 1/2", creating a tube.

6. Hold the overlapped bill with two hands. Place your thumbs on the top of the bills. Place your middle fingers at the back center of the bills.

7. Bend the bills in half toward the back using your middle fingers to push the bills inward. Line up the two corners of the bill.

8. Tape the fold together to secure the cookie shape using a strip of double-sided tape.

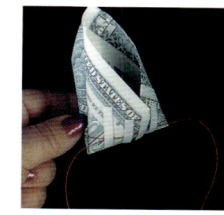

9. Cut a 20" length of red button thread. String the thread between the folded fortune cookie bills using a sewing needle. Tie a knot to secure the thread. Tape the thread to the back of the cookie using four strips of double-sided tape. Repeat steps 1 to 9 for ten cookies.

10. Cut a strip of red ribbon 70" in length. Cut a strip of gold ribbon 70" in length. Place a long strip of double-sided tape in the back center of the gold ribbon. Peel off the paper backing of the tape. Stick the gold ribbon onto the front center of the red ribbon. Cut the two ends of the ribbon to a "w" tip. Tape the fortune cookie stickers and the "Happiness" symbols evenly on both sides of the ribbon.

11. Sew the fortune cookie bills onto the ribbon using a sewing needle. Tie a knot in the back of the ribbon to secure the bills. White thread is used for this photo.

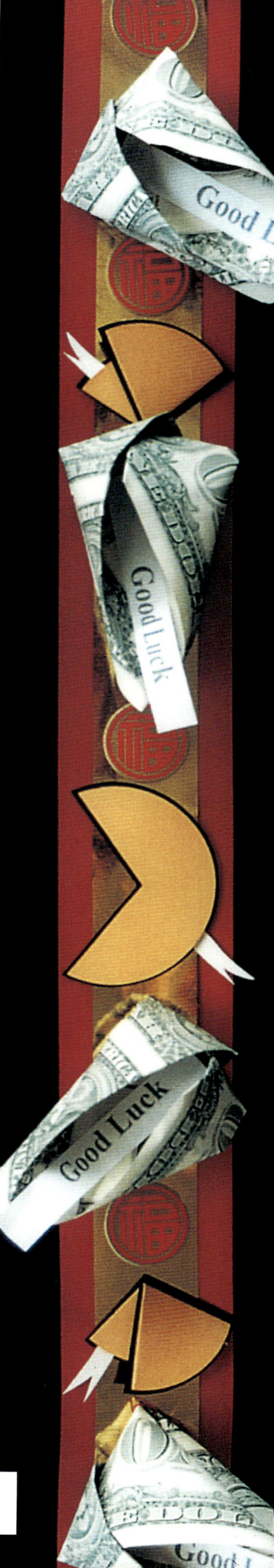

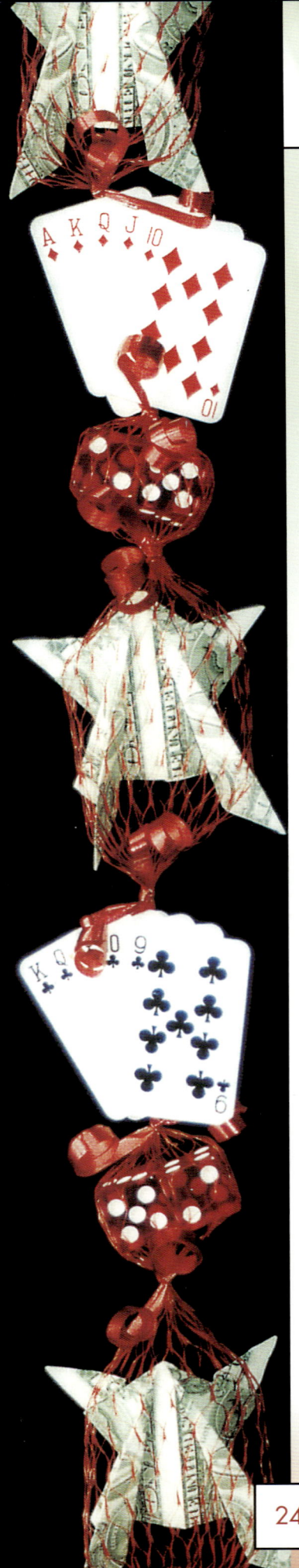

Frog Dollar Las Vegas Lei

Two bills make one frog. May substitute Las Vegas casino chips for the dice. Use something heavy to add weight to the lei.

Makes a 40" lei.

MATERIALS:

12 dollar bills, crisp
2 pks. playing cards, mini
1 glue gun and 4 glue
    sticks
2 yds. poly (net) tubing, red
6 pr. dice
7 yds. ribbon, curling,
    3/16", red
1 tape measure
1 scissors

1. Place double-sided tape along the bottom edge of the bill. Stick another bill onto the taped edge.

2. Fold the bottom left side of the bill up toward the top edge.

3. Fold the right edge of the taped bill inward against the edge of the formed triangle. Open all folds.

4. Place two small pieces of double-sided tape along the folded edge of the bill to keep the square secured. Fold the right edge over, along the formed crease.

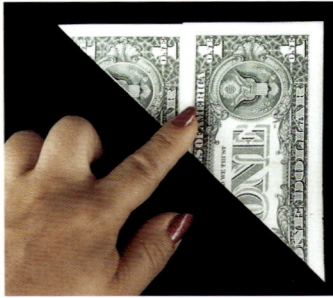

5. Fold the bottom left corner up, forming a triangle.

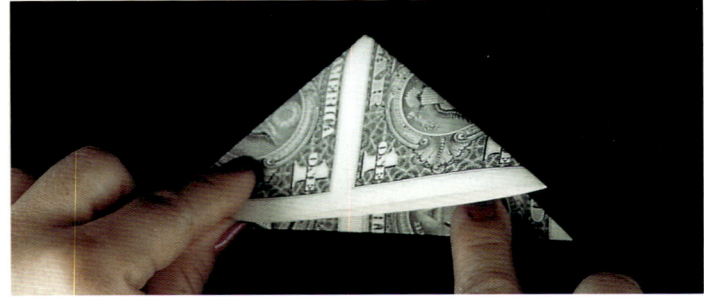

6. Flip and turn the bill. Bend the top corner of the bill forward, forming a smaller triangle. Open all folds.

7. Push in the two sides of the bill at the crease, forming an even point. Position the two "1s" of the bill in the front.

8. Fold the two bottom corners up to the top of the triangle tip.

9. Fold the two top triangles inward evenly toward the center.

10. Fold the two double triangles downward. Flip and turn the bill.

11. Fold the bottom two corners toward the center line.

12. Fold the two bottom points outward toward the outer edge.

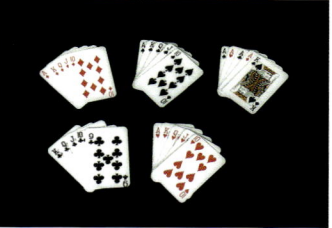

13. Glue the cards together, forming winning poker hands, using hot glue. Keep five extra cards for the back of the poker hands.

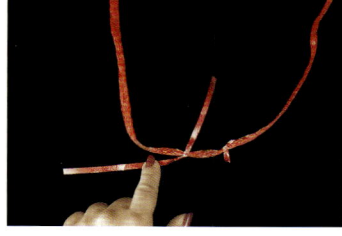

14. Cut a piece of tubing 70" in length. Cut two pieces of ribbon 10" in length. Tie a knot in the center of the tubing using the ribbon. Trim the ends of the ribbon. Tie another knot on the tubing 2" to the left of the trimmed knot, using a strip of ribbon. Do not trim the second ribbon.

15. Glue one set of cards to the center of the tubing, horizontally over the ribbon knot. Glue an extra card to the back of the cards to cover the glued mechanics.

16. Insert a pair of dice into the tubing with seven dots showing through the net. Tie a knot using a 10" strip of ribbon. Add a frog dollar into the tubing, back legs first. Tie a knot using a 10" strip of ribbon. Add another pair of dice into the tubing with seven dots showing through the net. Tie a knot using a 10" strip of ribbon. Tie a knot about 2" to the left of the last ribbon knot. Trim off the excess ribbon. Glue another set of cards vertically to the tubing covering the knot. Glue an extra card to the back to cover the glued mechanics. Continue adding the ribbon, frog, ribbon, dice, ribbon, cards glued vertically onto the trimmed ribbon, followed by a ribbon, and ending with a frog.

17. Repeat the same pattern on the opposite side of the lei. Tie the tubing ends with a double square knot to close the lei. Curl the ribbons with a scissors. Add a bow if desired.

Gerbera Daisy Dime Lei

Quick and easy to make. May use different silk flower petals. Great for birthdays and graduations. May use game tokens instead of the quarters.

Makes a 60" lei.

MATERIALS:

9 dimes

8 quarters

9 flowers, silk, gerbera daisies or similar

5 yds. ribbon, acetate, #9 (1-1/2"), gold

5 yds ribbon, acetate, #5 (7/8"), white

1 ft. clear plastic wrap

2-1/2 yds. tape, double-sided, 3/16"

3 yds. thread, button/carpet, white

1 hot glue gun and 3 glue sticks

1 tape measure

1 scissors

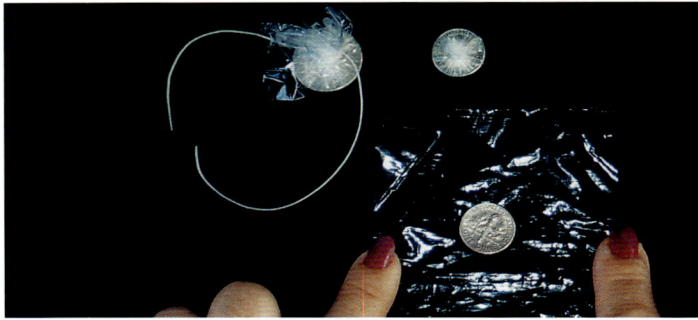

1. Cut a square piece of plastic wrap 3" x 3". Wrap a dime in the center of the plastic, facing the head down. Twist the plastic to tighten the slack. Tie a knot with thread to secure the dime. Trim off the excess thread and plastic. Continue for all dimes and quarters. Cut the plastic wrap 4" x 4" for the quarters.

2. Break apart the silk gerbera daisies by taking off the calyx.

3. Select the larger petal layer. Glue on the wrapped dime to the center of the gerbera daisy. Repeat steps 2 to 3 for all dimes.

4. Cut a piece of gold ribbon 60" in length. Cut a piece of white ribbon 60" in length. Tape the white ribbon to the gold ribbon using double-sided tape. Cut the two ends to a "w" tip. Overlap and glue the two ends of the ribbon together about 5" from the end.

5. Position the gerbera daisies and the quarters evenly on the ribbon. Start from the bottom of the ribbon. Glue the gerbera daisies and quarters to the ribbon.

Graduation Cap Dollar Lei

One bill makes one cap. Assorted colors of mini tassels may also be purchased by the yard as tassel trim. Trim the sharp tips of the Mylar graduation caps to smooth the edges. Hot glue is best to secure the diplomas to the ribbon.

Makes a 72" lei.

MATERIALS:

- 10 dollar bills, crisp
- 2 yds. ribbon, acetate, #9, (1-1/2"), blue
- 2 yds. ribbon, acetate, #5, (7/8"), white w/ blue graduation print
- 6 yds. tape, double-sided tape, 3/16"
- 2 yds. tape, single-sided, 3/4"
- 10 mini tassels, black (1 pack)
- 1 cardboard, thin, 2"x 10"
- 10 "diploma" computer printouts on copy paper
- 10 confetti scrapbook cutouts, large Mylar graduation caps, blue
- 10 sequins, 8 mm, black
- 1 hot glue gun and 3 glue sticks
- 1 tape measure
- 1 scissors

1. Cut a 2" x 2" square piece of cardboard. Crease along three borders of the bill. Slide the cardboard through the creased border.

2. Tape the edges of the bill to the cardboard using single-sided tape. Blue tape is used for this photo.

3. Fold the bill around the cardboard. Fold in the end of the bill. Tape the bill around the cardboard using double-sided tape. Show the eagle on the top of the cap.

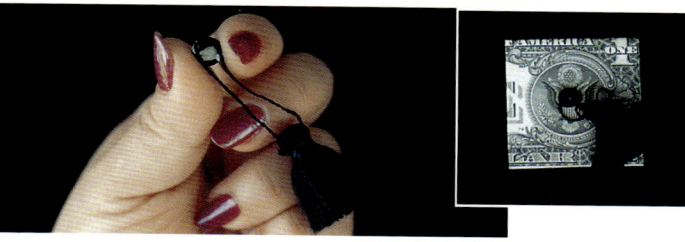

4. Make a small ball using double-sided tape. Stick the tassel cord under the sequin. Stick the sequin onto the middle of the folded bill. Repeat steps 1 to 4 for nine additional bills.

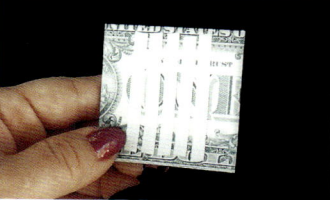

5. Place a lot of double-sided tape along the back of the dollar cap.

6. Print, cut, roll, and tape ten diploma signs from your computer.

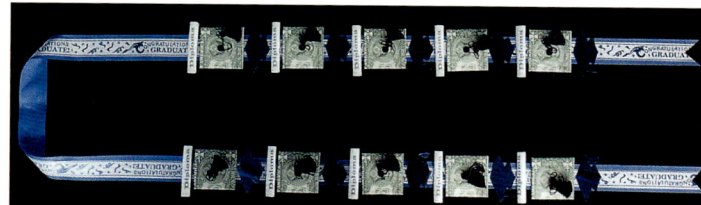

7. Cut a strip of #9 blue ribbon 72" in length. Cut a strip of #5 graduation ribbon 72" in length. Place a long strip of double-sided tape on the back of the graduation ribbon. Peel off the paper backing of the tape. Stick on the graduation ribbon to the front center of the blue ribbon. Cut the two ends of the ribbon to a "w" tip. Place and tape the dollar caps, diplomas, and confetti onto the ribbon, spaced evenly. Start 5" from the ends of the ribbon.

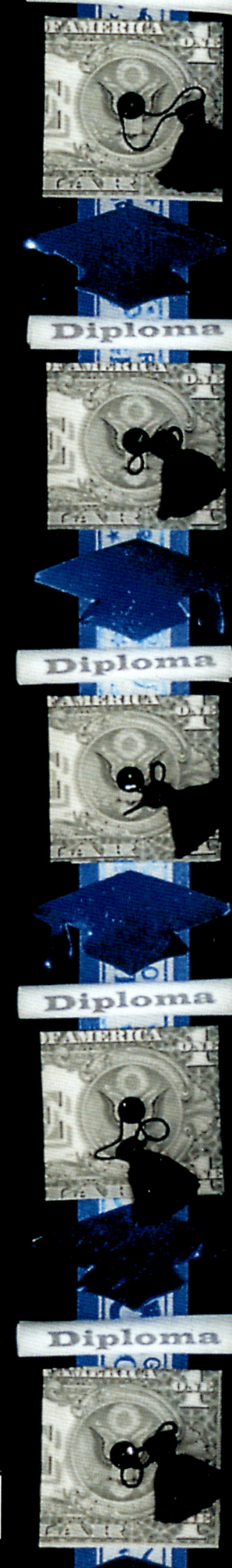

Heart Dollar Love Lei

For a taller person use a longer ribbon. One bill makes one heart. Optional: To better secure the bill, sew it on the ribbon. See page 13, Crane "Long Life" Dollar Lei. Visit www.free-clipart-pictures.net for free clipart for the "love" prints.

Makes a 70" lei.

MATERIALS:

- 10 dollar bills, crisp
- 2 yds. ribbon, acetate, #16 (2-1/4"), red
- 2 yds. ribbon, acetate, #9 (1-1/2"), white
- 2 yds. tape, double-sided, 3/4"
- 6 picks Styrofoam hearts or similar
- 4 love clipart prints on cardstock paper
- 10 stickers, hearts
- 1 glue gun and 2 glue sticks
- 1 tape measure
- 1 scissors

1. Fold the four corners of the bill inward to the center, forming 2 points.

2. Fold the top and bottom edge of the bill inward ½".

3. Fold the bill in half to form a crease. Open the fold.

4. Fold the right side of the bill upward at the center crease.

5. Fold the left side of the bill upward at the center crease, forming the heart shape. Flip the bill.

6. Fold the two top points of the heart down. Tape the points down.

7. Add double-sided tape to the back of the heart bills. May add thread to the back of the taped bills for added security. See page 13, Crane "Long Life" Dollar Lei for sewing on the bill.

8. Print and cut out four "love" clipart prints from a computer, using cardstock paper.

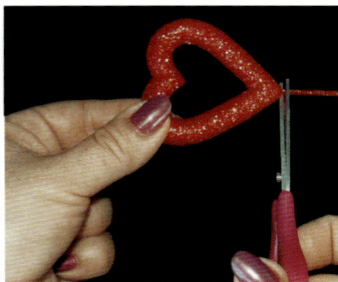

9. Cut the styrofoam heart off the pick.

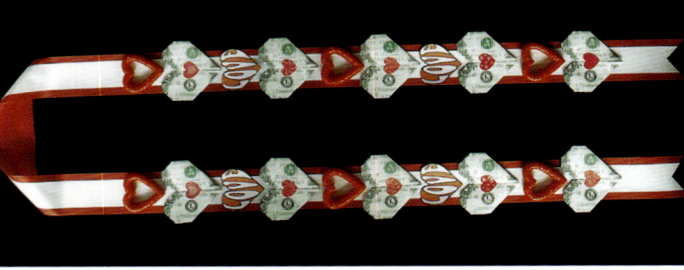

10. Cut strips of red and white ribbon 70" in length. Tape the white ribbon to the red ribbon using a long strip of double-sided tape. Cut the two ends of the ribbon to a "w" tip. Place the heart bills, the Styrofoam hearts, and the "love" clipart evenly on both sides of the ribbon to determine the pattern. Tape the heart bills and "love" clipart to the ribbon. Glue the Styrofoam hearts to the ribbon. Stick the heart stickers to the heart bills.

Hibiscus Dollar Lei

Three bills make one hibiscus. Visit **www.hulahlahs.com** *for the red hibiscus flower laser-cut prints.*

Makes a 72" lei including the streamers.

MATERIALS:

3 dollar bills, crisp

6 dimes

1 text paper, red, 8-1/2" x 11"

1 stamen, silk hibiscus flower

2 hibiscus, pre-assembled paper cutouts, stickers, or similar (5 flowers)

2 yds. ribbon, acetate, #9 (1-1/2"), white

2 yds. ribbon, acetate, #5 (7/8"), red

1 florist wire, #24

1 florist wire, #22

12 in. floral tape, 3/16", green

1 wire cutter

1 ft. floral tape, dark green, 1/2"

3 yds. thread, carpet/button, white

1 sewing needle

1 ft. plastic wrap

1 pen (optional)

1 glue gun and 1 glue stick

2-1/8 yds. tape, double-sided 3/16"

1 tape measure

1 scissors

1. Cut a piece of paper 4 -3/4" x 2".

2. Cut the two ends of the paper to a round shape using fancy-cut scissors.

3. Tape the red piece of paper on the center of the bill using a 1/2" piece of double-sided tape at each end of the paper.

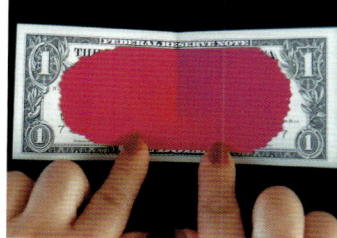

4. Fold the bill in half to crease. Open the fold.

5. Gather the bills together in the center along the crease by pinching inward, forming two upward-facing petals. Repeat steps 1 to 5 for two additional bills.

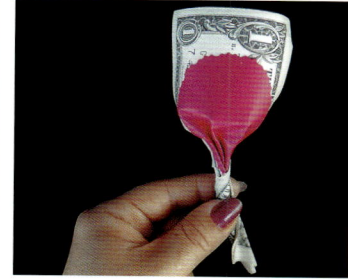

6. Twist half of the bill to form one petal for the third bill.

7. Gather the three bills together to form the flower. Place the two long bills in a criss-cross position. Add in the third bill with one petal.

8. Wire the bills together in the center while holding the bills in place. Place the extra twisted petal downward to form the stem. Use the #22 (thicker) wire.

9. Remove the stamen from one silk hibiscus flower. Wrap a wire around the bottom of the stamen. Cover the wire using floral tape. The photo shows the stamen taken from a hibiscus hair clip. Use the #24 (thinner) wire.

10. Add in the wired stamen to the center of the blossom.

11. Squeeze the bills together at the base of the wired stem. Cover the stem mechanics using floral tape. Cut off the wired stem, leaving about 4-1/2" for the stem. Do not cut the stem of the bill.

12. Curl the ends of the bills backward using a pen. Curl the wired stem using a pen.

13. Wrap six dimes in a 3" x 3" plastic wrap. Tie the top of the wrap using a 7" thread. Trim off the excess wrap and thread.

14. Cut apart the hibiscus paper flowers.

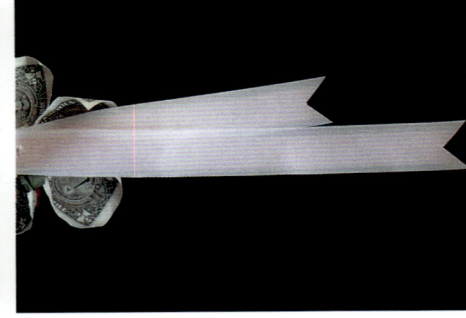

15. Cut strips of white and red ribbon, 70" in length. Tape the ribbons to the floor to work. Tape the red ribbon onto the top center of the white ribbon using a long strip of double-sided tape. Cut the two ends of the ribbon to a "w" tip. Cross the ribbon ends to close the lei. Overlap 12" for the longer ribbon and 9" for the shorter ribbon. Tack down the overlapped ribbon to secure the ribbon shape. Place the money hibiscus, hibiscus paper flowers, and wrapped dimes evenly on both sides of the lei to determine a pattern. Glue down the paper flowers and wrapped dimes.

16. Sew the money hibiscus flower to the ribbon over the tack. Trim off the excess thread.

Ilima Penny Maile Lei

*Use fifty pennies for a 60"
maile lei. One standard
roll of cellophane is 60".
For a longer maile lei, use
a longer cellophane strip
or join the strips together.*

MATERIALS:

- 50 pennies
- 1 maile lei, silk, 60" or longer
- 5 ft. cellophane film, orange
- 11 yds. ribbon, curling, 3/16", orange
- 1 clip
- 1 tape measure
- 1 scissors

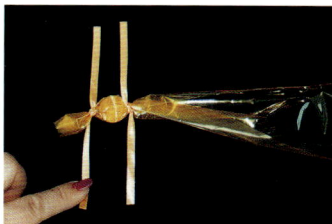

1. Cut a strip of cellophane 60" x 3". Wrap a penny in the cellophane, forming a tube to secure the penny. Tie before and after the penny using a 6" length of ribbon. Rotate from front to back when tying the cellophane.

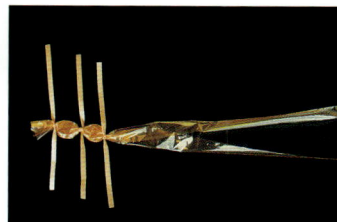

2. Wrap another penny in the cellophane. Tie a knot after the penny on the opposite side of the first penny. Keep all pennies facing the same direction. Continue until all fifty pennies are wrapped.

3. Curl all ribbon ends except the first and last ribbon ties using scissors.

4. Anchor the center of the penny lei to the center of the maile lei using a clip.

5. Twine the penny lei around the maile lei on both sides evenly.

6. Anchor the ends of the penny lei to the maile using the first and last ribbon ties of the penny lei.

7. Cut and tie seven strips of 6" ribbon evenly around the maile lei to anchor the penny lei to the maile lei. Place the first anchor in the middle of the maile lei.

8. Curl the anchor ribbons using a scissors.

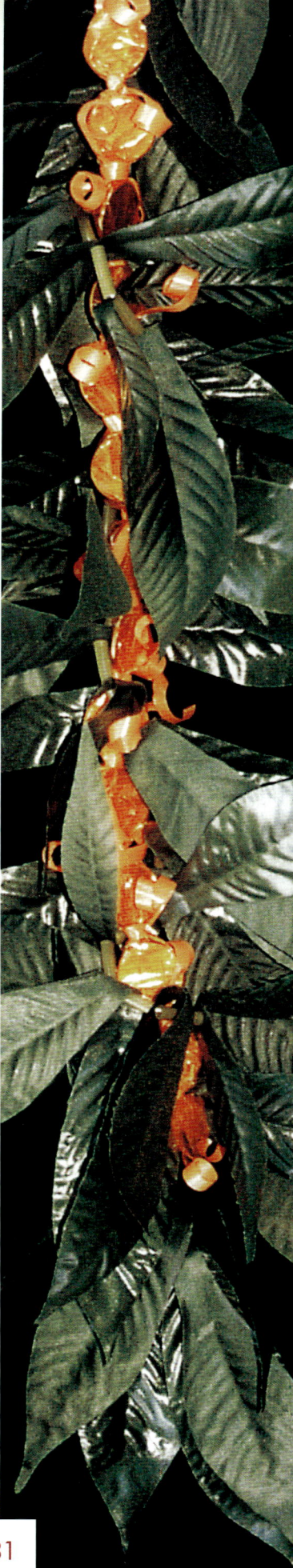

Las Vegas Chip Blackjack Lei

Glossy cards are best for this lei. Great for people who love going to Las Vegas. May use silver dollars, $1.00 Las Vegas tokens, or plastic poker chips to cut cost. Use four chips for the back of the neck area.

Makes a 50" lei.

MATERIALS:

10 casino chips
4 pks. cards, glossy
2 yds. poly tubing, 2" wide
5 yds. ribbon, curling, 3/16", red
1 roll tape, double-sided, 3/4"
1 tape measure
1 scissors

1. Tape together fourteen sets of blackjack hands using double-sided tape. Be sure the sets line up when placing them back-to-back.

2. Cut a piece of plastic tubing 70" in length. Tape the tubing to the back of a set of cards using double-sided tape. Add additional tape to secure the cards. Peel off the paper backing of the tape. Stick another set of cards to the back. Line the cards up evenly.

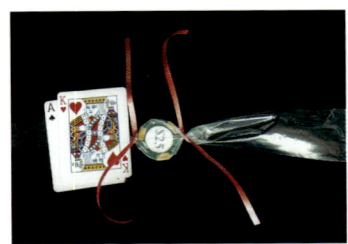
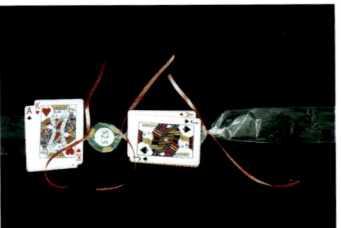

3. Tie a knot after the cards using a 10" ribbon. Insert a chip into the tubing. Tie a knot after the chip using a 10" ribbon.

4. Tape two sets of cards back-to-back on the tubing using double-sided tape. Face the cards horizontally on the tubing. Tie a knot after the cards.

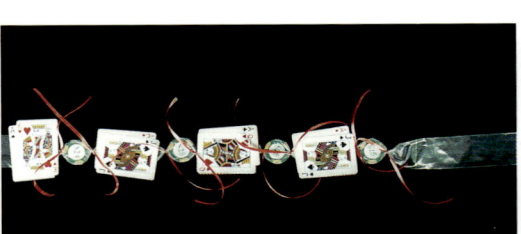
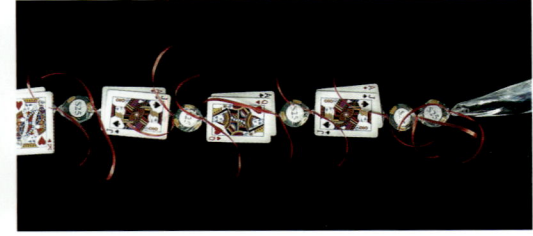

5. Insert a chip into the tubing. Tie a knot after the chip using a 10" ribbon. Repeat steps 4 and 5 for two additional sets of cards and chips.

6. Insert another chip into the tubing. Tie a knot after the chip using a 10" ribbon.

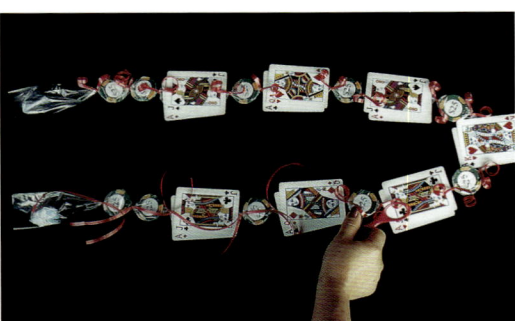
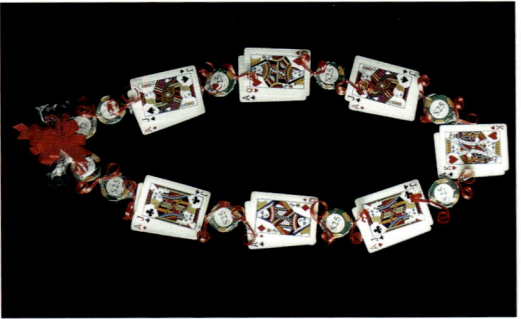

7. Repeat the identical card and chip pattern for the opposite side of the tubing. Face the cards in the opposite direction, facing upward. Curl the ribbons using a scissors.

8. Tie a knot to join the tubing. Add a bow if desired.

Long Dollar Graduation Lei

May use computer printout on cardstock paper to substitute for centerpiece fountain trim. Working on the floor is best. Tape the long dollar and ribbons to the floor to hold them steady.

Makes a 68" lei.

MATERIALS:

- 10 dollar bills, crisp
- 6 yds. tape, double-sided 3/16"
- 1 graduation centerpiece cascade fountain or similar for 18 to 20 decoration cut-outs
- 8 ft. ribbon, acetate, #3 (5/8"), yellow
- 8 ft. ribbon, acetate, #3 (5/8"), purple
- 2 graduation plush toys or similar
- 1 tape measure
- 1 scissors

1. Place double-sided tape along the right edge of the bill. Continue this step for a total of nine bills. The last bill will not need taping.

2. Peel off the paper backing of the tape. Stick another bill to the taped edge to join the bills. Continue until all bills are joined.

3. Cut a strip of yellow ribbon 80" in length. Cut a strip of purple ribbon 80" in length. Add the double-sided tape to the back center of each strip of ribbon. Start and end the tape about 10" from the ends of the ribbon. Keep the ribbon ends free for streamers. Tape the two ribbon strips along the center of the long, joined bill, leaving 10" of ribbon on each end for the streamers.

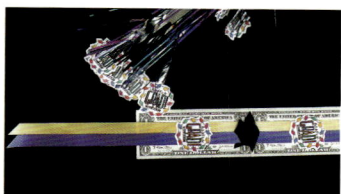

4. Tape on the decorative hats and trim to the long, joined bills spaced evenly using double-sided tape. Bend the lei in half. Tape the second half of the trim in the opposite direction.

5. Tie the yellow and purple streamers into a knot at the ends of the bill strip.

6. Tear the yellow and purple 18" ribbons in half to create two thinner ribbon strips. Insert the ribbon strips into the streamer knots.

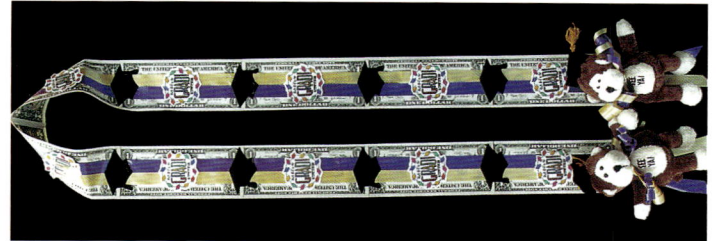

7. Add in the plush toy. Tie a knot in front of the toy. Curl the ends of the thin ribbon. Repeat steps 5 to 7 for the other end of the lei. Trim the streamers evenly.

Micronesian Dollar Lei

One bill makes one flower bud. Must use button/carpet thread. Lei twine does not slide through the taped opening. Flatten all creases using a pen.

Makes a 33" lei.

MATERIALS:

50 dollar bills, crisp

2 yds. tape, double-sided 3/16"

3 yds. thread, button/carpet, white

1 sewing needle

1 toothpick

1 pen

1 tape measure

1 scissors

1. Fold the bill in half lengthwise.

2. Fold the top and bottom sides of the bill toward the center.

3. Fold the bill in half lengthwise.

4. Fold the bill in half widthwise. Open the fold.

5. Fold the two ends of the bill inward, creasing just after the "1" in the corners of the bill.

6. Tape along the inside of one side of the bill.

7. Stick the two sides of the bill together evenly. Flatten the bill using a pen.

8. Cut thread 104" in length. Tie a knot 6" from the open end of the thread. Attach a toothpick to the knotted end of the thread to secure the first bill. Sew the bills onto the thread through the space next to the fold.

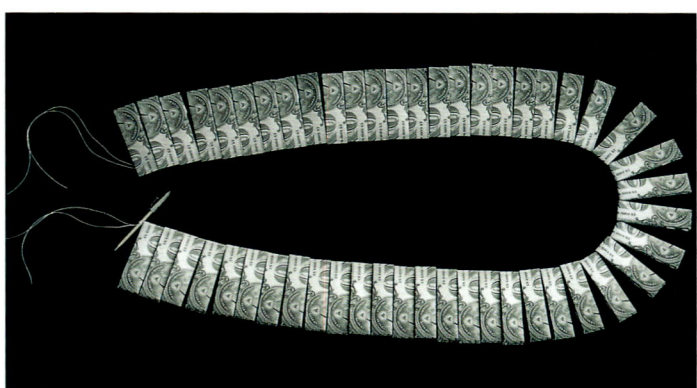

9. Position all bills facing in the same direction. Tie a knot to close the lei. Trim off the excess thread. Add a bow if desired.

Owl Dollar Graduation Lei

One bill makes one owl. May use one graduation cap necklace by repositioning the cap beads.

Makes a 70" lei.

Owl money origami design by Jodi Fukumoto.

MATERIALS:

- 10 dollar bills, crisp
- 2 graduation cap necklaces, gold
- 1 piece paper stock, 8-1/2" x 11", purple
- 1/3 yd. tassel trim, purple or 8 tassels
- 8 acrylic amethyst stones, 7mm, flat back, purple
- 2 yds. ribbon, acetate, #9 (1-1/2"), purple
- 2 yds. ribbon, acetate, #5 (7/8"), white w/ gold graduation print
- 2 yds. tape, double-sided 3/16"
- 2 yds. strong, crafting double-sided tape, 3/4"
- 1 glue gun and 3 glue sticks
- 4 yds. thread, button/ carpet, purple or similar
- 1 sewing needle
- 1 ruler
- 1 tape measure
- 1 scissors

1. Fold the bill in half widthwise. Turn the bill.

2. Create a point. Fold the open ends of the bill downward, toward the center, on both sides. Flip the bill.

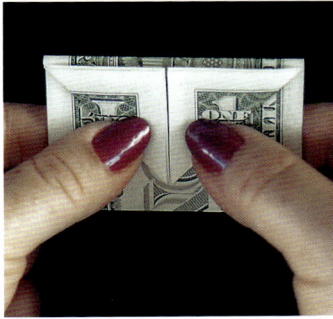

3. Fold the top of the bill forward, creasing 1/16" above the folded triangle.

4. Fold the two top corners of the bill downward, to form two square eyes.

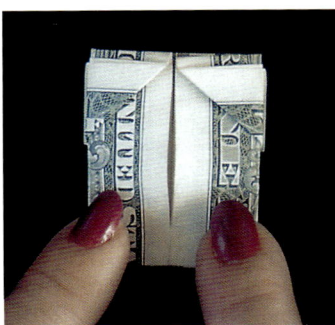

5. Fold the two sides of the bill toward the back, creasing after the owl's eye. Flip the bill.

6. Lift the beak of the owl. Fold it upward and then downward to form the beak. Flip the bill.

7. Fold the two bottom sides of the bill inward toward the center, forming the triangle chin of the owl.

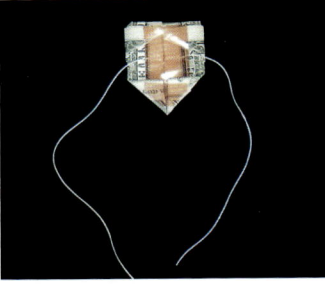

8. Cut a piece of thread 12" in length. Cut a piece of strong double-sided tape 1" in length. Stick the tape to the opened owl's head. Peel off the paper backing of the tape. Close the owl head flaps of the bill. Stick on another piece of tape over the thread. Tape down the two side folds of the back of the owl, leaving the two threads for tying. Add a small piece of tape to secure the bottom triangular folds down. Repeat steps 1 to 8 for nine additional owl bills.

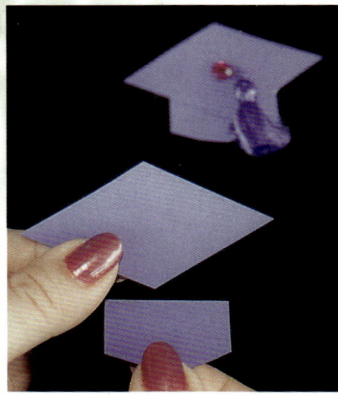

9. Make two patterns for the graduation cap from card stock paper using a ruler. Trace the pattern, making eight diamond-shaped pieces for the top of the hat and eight rectangular-shaped pieces for the bottom of the hat. Glue or tape the hat pieces together. Glue a tassel and a flat amethyst stone in the center of the graduation cap to secure the tassel.

10. Cut the graduation cap beads off the necklace.

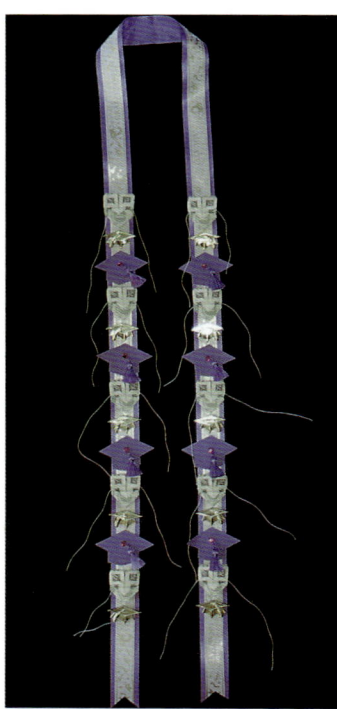

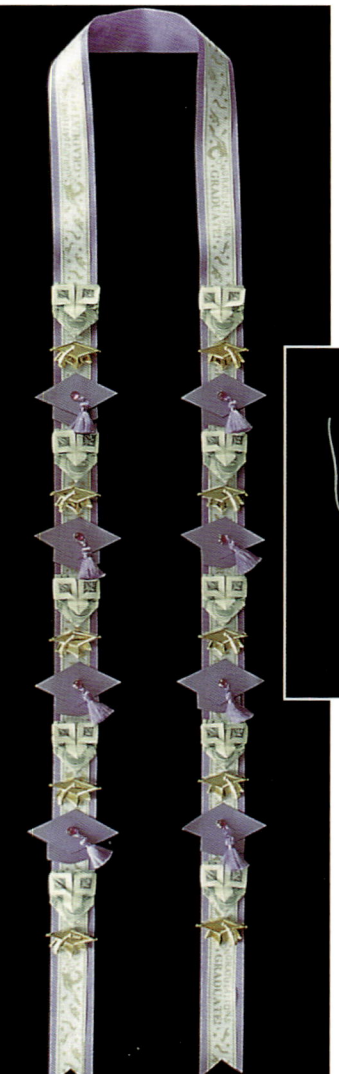

11. Cut a strip of purple ribbon 70" in length. Cut a piece of white ribbon 70" in length. Stick the white ribbon onto the top center of the purple ribbon using the thin double-sided tape. Cut the two ends of the ribbon to a "w" tip. Place the ten owls, ten cap beads, and eight paper caps evenly on each side of the ribbon. Start with the lowest hat bead or owl 4" from the ends of the ribbon. Glue the cap beads and paper caps onto the ribbon. Peel off the paper backing of the tape from the owls. Stick the owls onto the ribbon.

12. Sew the owls to the ribbon to secure the bills. Tie a knot in the back of the ribbon. Trim off the excess thread.

Plumeria Dollar Pikake Lei

One bill makes one plumeria flower. Great for a 21st birthday lei using $21.00. Fold all corners neatly and perfectly for this design.

Makes a 40" lei.

Plumeria money origami design by Jodi Fukumoto.

MATERIALS:

- 21 dollar bills, crisp
- 1 lei, silk, double pikake w/ rosebuds or similar
- 14 leaves, silk philodendron
- 2 yds. double-sided tape, 3/4", strong
- 7 wires, florist #22 or similar
- 1 roll tape, floral, green
- 1 glue gun and 3 glue sticks
- 1 wire cutter
- 1 ruler
- 1 scissors

1. Place the bill facing to the right. Fold the top of the bill down leaving exactly 1" of the bill uncovered.

2. Fold the 1" uncovered flap upward against the inside edge of the fold.

3. Fold the bill in half lengthwise to crease. Open the fold.

4. Open the wide fold, keeping the narrow fold. Fold the two corners of the narrow side of the bill toward the center, forming a point.

5. Fold the two corners of the other end of the bill toward the center, forming a point.

6. Fold the bill in half.

7. Fold the two top corners of the straight side of the bill toward the center, forming a point. Open these two folds.

8. Tuck in and crease the left and right sides of the bill, creating a triangle tip.

9. Fold the top flap of the bill upward in half.

10. Fold the two side edges of the top layer of the bill upward to the top point.

11. Place your pointers in each pocket of the triangle fold created in step 10. Press to flatten forming petals.

12. Pinch and create the triangle ends of the bill together matching up the edges and points.

13. Bend the excess tip toward the outside of the formed flower.

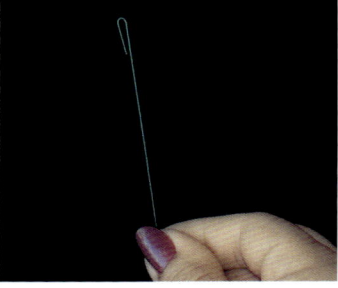

14. Cut a piece of wire 6" in length. Form a small hook on one end of the wire.

15. Tape the hook to the inside of the flower using double-sided tape. Peel off the paper backing of the tape. Tape the bill together.

16. Tape the flap down, using strong double-sided tape.

17. Curl the petal tips outward using your fingers or a pen. Repeat steps 1 to 17 for twenty additional flowers.

18. Bind three plumeria flowers together with floral tape.

19. Cut off all the silk roses from the pikake lei.

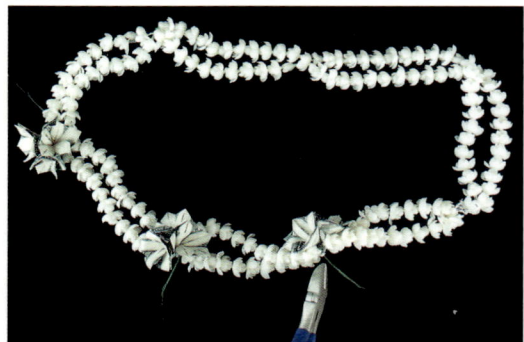

20. Wrap the wired plumeria clusters around the lei where the roses were. Trim the wire using a wire cutter. Add floral tape if needed to cover any sharp wire edges.

21. Glue the two philodendron silk leaves to the pikake lei under each plumeria cluster.

Present Dollar Birthday Lei

One bill makes one present. Visit **www.free-clipart-pictures.net** for the red present clipart. A strong double-sided tape is enough to secure the bills to the ribbon. For added security, sew the bills onto the ribbon. See page 13 for adding thread to the back of the bill. When taking apart this lei, remove the tape slowly and carefully.

Makes a 70" lei.

MATERIALS:

- 6 dollar bills, crisp
- 8 party horns
- 6 presents, computer clipart
- 6 confetti, large, birthday cake, green or similar
- 2 ribbons, pre-made, curly, streamer stick-on or similar
- 5 ft. ribbon, acetate, #9 (1-1/2"), gold
- 3 yds. tape, transparent or similar
- 6 yds. tape, double-sided, strong, 3/4"
- 5 yds. ribbon, curling, rainbow
- 6 pcs cardboard, thin, 2"x 2"
- 1 glue gun and 4 to 5 glue sticks
- 1 sheet of cardstock, white
- 1 tape measure
- 1 scissors

1. Cut a 2" x 2" square piece of cardboard. Crease along three borders of the bill. Slide the cardboard through the creased border.

2. Tape the edges of the bill to the cardboard using single-sided tape. Blue tape is used for this photo.

3. Fold the bill around the cardboard. Fold in the end of the bill. Tape the bill around the cardboard using double-sided tape. Show the eagle on the top of the cap.

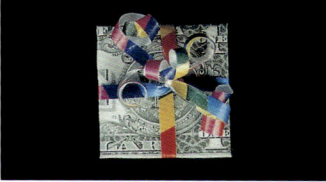

4. Tie a ribbon around the dollar present. Curl the ends of the ribbon using a scissors. Repeat steps 1 to 4 for all bills.

5. Print and cut out six birthday present clipart images from your computer. Use cardstock paper.

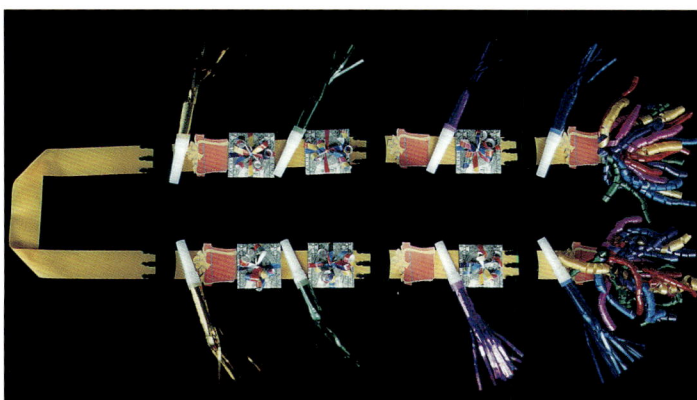

6. Cut a strip of gold ribbon 60" in length. Cut the two ends of the ribbon to a "w" tip. Glue the two curly streamer ribbons onto the front bottom ends of the gold ribbon. Position the six dollar presents, horns, confetti cakes, and clipart presents to the ribbon evenly. Place double-sided tape onto the back of the dollar presents, clipart presents, and confetti cake. Peel off the paper backing of the tape. Stick the dollar presents, confetti cakes, and clipart presents to the ribbon. Use hot glue to secure the party horns to the ribbon.

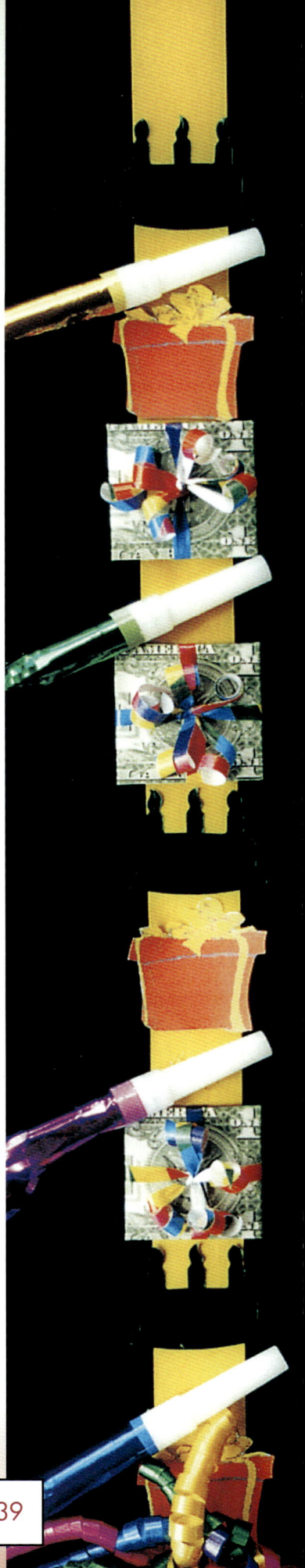

Rose Dollar Lei

Two bills make one rose. Substitute colored paper for bills to cut cost. Use them in the center of the rose.

Makes a 40" lei.

MATERIALS:

72 dollar bills, crisp

1 roll tape, double-sided, 3/16"

1 roll transparent tape, 1/2"

36 poly calyx 1-1/2 x 2"

3 yds. thread, button craft, white

1 sewing needle, long

1 pen (covered)

1 tape measure

1 scissors

1. Fold the bill in half lengthwise to crease. Open the bill.

2. Fold the two sides of the bill inward to the crease.

3. Fold the bill in half lengthwise. Repeat steps 1 to 3 for a second bill.

4. Open up the last fold of the bills. Tape along the right edge of one of the folded bills using double-sided tape.

5. Stick the second bill onto the first bill along the taped edge. Place the bills facing the same direction.

6. Fold the attached bills in half lengthwise on the existing crease.

7. Hold 1" from one end of the bill strip. Fold the two sides of the end of the bill inward to create a tubular stem.

8. Hold the stem end of the bill. Bend the bill strip over your thumb to the left.

9. Wrap the bill backward around your thumb. Pinch the bill to hold it in place.

10. Make a backward and downward fold. Twist the stem in your left hand to the right while wrapping the bill strip in your right hand toward the left.

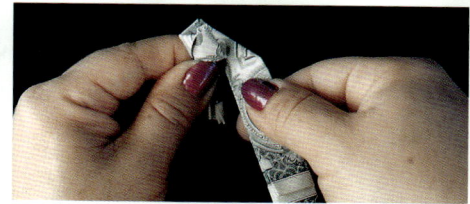

11. Make another backward and downward fold.

12. Twist the stem to the right while wrapping the dollar strip around creating the rose petals. Stop when you have twisted up to the end of the downward fold. Continue this step with the backward and downward fold while twisting the stem to the right. Continue this step until 1" from the end of the strip. Pinch the petals together to shape the rose.

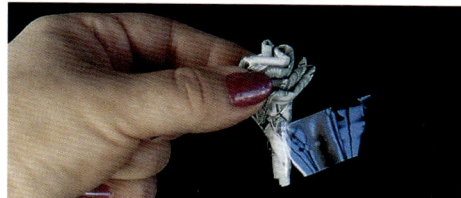

13. Wrap the remaining end of the dollar strip around the stem. Keep the stem thin. Tape down the end of the bill by wrapping a piece of transparent tape around the stem to secure the rose for stringing.

14. Cut off the base of the calyx to enlarge the opening.

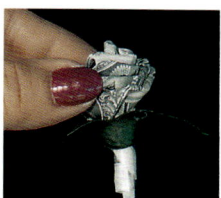

15. Insert the rose stem into the calyx.

16. Open the rose using a closed pen.

17. Cut a strip of thread 104" in length. Fold the thread in half. Tie a knot 6" from the open end of the thread. Hook on a lei needle. If using a sewing needle, thread the needle before tying the knot. Pierce the roses onto the needle from the top of the flower through the stem. Do not pierce the bills. Pull the roses down to the thread knot. Insert the stems into the previously strung flowers to hide the taped ends.

18. Continue until all roses are strung. Tie a knot to join the lei. Add a bow if desired.

Rosebud Dollar Quarter Lei

One bill makes one rosebud for the top of the lei and one rosebud for the bottom of the lei. Use colored paper or paper in school colors to reduce cost.

Makes a 40" lei.

MATERIALS:

30 dollar bills, crisp

30 quarters

1 roll tape, double-sided, 3/16"

6 yds. curling ribbon, 3/16", green

1 pen

1 tape measure

1 scissors

1. Fold the two sides of the back of the bill inward about 3/4".

2. Place a quarter in the center of the bill.

3. Place double-sided tape along the two edges of the bill. Peel off the paper backing. Seal in the quarter.

4. Pinch gently and twist the two ends of the bill, securing the quarter and twisting the two ends in the opposite direction.

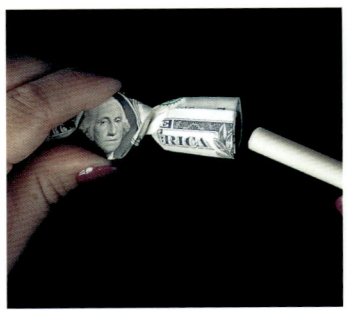

5. Open the two ends of the bill using the back of a pen.

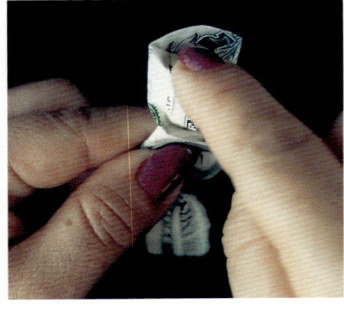

6. Push in the four edges of the folded bill, forming a rosebud.

7. Place one bill over another bill just below the rosebud. Tie the bills together under the first quarter using a 7" strip of ribbon. Continue steps 1 to 7. Continue for all thirty bills.

8. Curl the ribbon ends using a scissors.

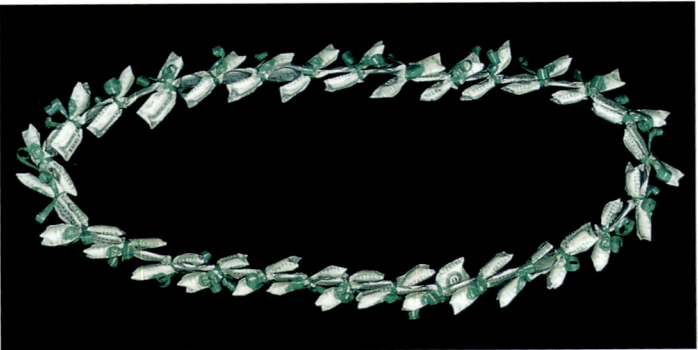

9. Tie the ends together to join the lei.

Tahitian Gardenia Dollar Lei

Three bills make one gardenia flower. This flower usually has seven to eight petals, but six petals are common.

*Visit **www.hulahlahs.com** for the Tahitian gardenia (tiare) laser-cut prints.*

Makes a 70" lei.

Cut out the flowers individually for a thinner lei.

MATERIALS:

- 18 dollar bills, crisp
- 4 Tahitian gardenia flowers, laser cut-outs or similar
- 12 pcs. rhinestone flowers, 14 mm, pink
- 12 pcs. rhinestone flowers, 14 mm, peridot green
- 2 yds. ribbon, acetate, #9 (1-1/2"), azelea pink
- 2 yds. ribbon, acetate, #5 (7/8"), white
- 2 yds. tape, double-sided 3/16"
- 2 yds. thread, button/carpet, pink or white
- 2 florist wires, #26, green or similar
- 1 sewing needle
- 1 hot glue gun and 4 glue sticks
- 1 wire cutter
- 1 pen or pencil
- 1 tape measure
- 1 scissors

1. Fold the two sides of the bill inward 1-5/16".

2. Fold the bill in half, lengthwise to form a crease. Open the fold.

3. Fold the four corners of the bill inward toward the center crease.

4. Fold the top and bottom of the bill inward toward the center crease.

5. Fold the bill in half lengthwise.

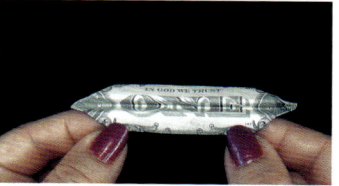

6. Fold the two open edges of the bill down toward the bottom edge of the bill, forming an accordion pattern into fourths. Repeat steps 1 to 6 for two additional bills.

7. Fold the three bills in half widthwise to form a crease.

8. Cut the wire into thirds. Tie a piece of wire around the center of the three folded bills. Place the two bills on the outside facing the same direction. Place the center bill facing the opposite direction. Twist the wire tight, securing the three bills.

9. Cut off the excess wire using a wire cutter. Use the back of a pen or pencil to flatten down the wire against the flower. Tie a 10" thread over the wire. Leave the thread long. Add double-sided tape to the back of the bills. Place the tape over the thread.

10. Cut pieces of pink and white ribbon 70" in length. Tape the white ribbon onto the center of the pink ribbon using a 70" strip of double-sided tape. Cut the ends to a "w" tip. Position the three money flowers, two Tahitian gardenia flower cutouts, six pink rhinestone flowers, and six green rhinestone flowers evenly on both sides of the ribbon. Start 3" from the ends of the ribbon.

11. Peel off the paper backing of the tape. Stick and sew the money flowers to the ribbon using a sewing needle. Tie a knot in the back of the ribbon. Trim off the excess ribbon. Glue the Tahitian gardenia cutouts and rhinestone flowers evenly on each side of the ribbon.

Ti-Leaf Dollar Orchid Lei

One bill makes one leaf. This lei can be kept open-ended or glued, tied or sewn together to make a closed lei. For a taller recipient, add 15" to 20" to each side of the twisted ribbon strands in step 8. The ten leaflet ribbons will stay the same. May use 30 dendrobium orchids for better coverage.

Makes a 58" lei.

MATERIALS:

10 dollar bills, crisp

6 yds. ribbon, acetate, #5 (7/8"), basil green or similar

4 florist wires, #26, cloth stem or similar

1 roll floral tape, dark green, 1/2"

20 silk flowers, dendrobium orchids or similar

1 glue gun and 5 glue sticks

1 tape measure

1 scissors

1. Fold the bill in half widthwise.

2. Fold the two sides of the bill down toward the center crease.

3. Fold the bill in half.

4. Fold the two sides of the bill, making 1/8" folds in an accordion pattern. Start the first fold backward to create the white tip of the leaf.

5. Cut the wire into thirds. Wrap a piece of wire three times around the stem of the leaf. Twist the wire with your fingernails to secure the leaf.

6. Tape the wire to the leaf using floral tape.

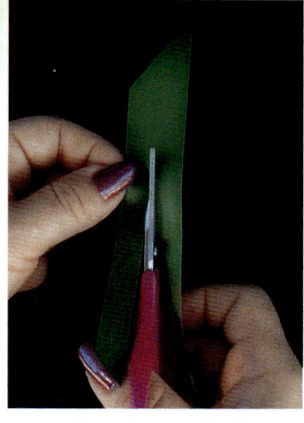

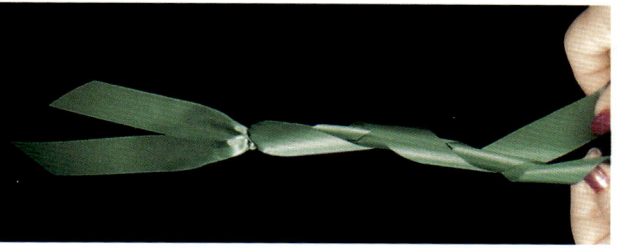

7. Cut five 6" strips of ribbon for the leaflets. Cut the ribbon in half lengthwise.

8. Cut a strip of ribbon 80" in length. Cut a strip of ribbon 70" in length. Tie the 80" and 70" ribbon strips together, leaving 6" from one end. Tape the knotted end of the ribbon to the floor. Hold the long ribbon in your left hand. Hold the short ribbon in your right hand. Twist the long ribbon to the right while wrapping the short ribbon around the twisted ribbon toward the left. Keep the twisted ribbons fairly tight. Continue until the ribbons are all twisted. Stretch the short ribbon to create the longest lei possible.

9. Tie a knot 6" from the end of the ribbons to secure the twist.

10. Insert the short ribbon strips into every third opening of the twisted lei.

11. Add five dollar leaves onto each side of the lei. Attach the dollar leaves onto the lei, wrapping the wire over the ten strips of ribbon to anchor it.

12. Glue on 2 silk flowers to the lei next to the dollar leaves to cover the wire and tape mechanics. Do not glue the bills.

Wedding Cake Dollar Lei

One bill makes one wedding cake. Great lei for a wedding shower. Use a longer ribbon for a taller recipient.

Makes a 72" lei including the streamers.

MATERIALS:

- 5 dollar bills, crisp
- 2 yds. ribbon, acetate #16 (2-1/4"), white
- 2 yds. tape, double-sided, 3/4"
- 2 cake cutouts/stickers or similar
- 7 double-bell stickers or similar
- 2 pkgs. mobile phone sticker strips, pearl/ yellow or similar
- 1 pkg. confetti, embossed, double-bells, silver
- 1 tape measure
- 1 scissors

1. Fold the right side of the bill inward at the border. Flip the bill.

2. Fold the bill downward and then upward, overlapping the "o" and "e" in "one." Flip the bill.

3. Fold in the two sides of the left side of the bill, creasing the corners to form two triangles.

4. Fold the left side of the bill downward and then upward, creasing at the half circle mark on the bill.

5. Fold the two sides of the top tier of the cake inward 1/8", creasing the corners forming two triangles.

6. Fold back the three white borders of the bottom tier of the cake. Flip the bill.

7. Tape on the bells and stickers strips to decorate the bill.

8. Place double-sided tape on the back of the bill.

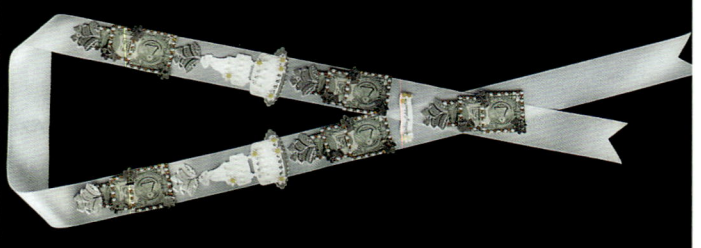

9. Cut a strip of ribbon 70" in length. Cut the two ends of the ribbon to a "w" tip. Cross the ribbon ends to close the lei. Overlap 12" for the longer end and 9" for the shorter end of the ribbon. Tape the overlapped ribbon to secure the ribbon shape using double-sided tape. Tape the cake bills, wedding cake, and bell stickers evenly on both sides of the lei.

Woven Ball Dollar Lei

Each ball is made using four dollar bills. May substitute school color paper for dollar bills to cut cost.

Makes a 40" lei with thirty-six woven balls.

Makes a 36" lei with thirty-two woven balls.

MATERIALS:

144 dollar bills, crisp

3 yds. tape, double-sided, 3/16"

1 tweezers

1 pen or pencil

3 yds. lei twine or carpet/ button thread, white

1 needle, yarn, tapestry or similar (blunt)

1 toothpick

1 tape measure

1 scissors

1. Fold the bottom third of the bill upward lengthwise.

2. Fold the top third of the bill down lengthwise.

3. Fold the bill in half lengthwise. Flatten the folded bill using a pen. Repeat steps 1 to 3 for three additional bills.

4. Make two double-dollar strips. Tape two folded bills together to lengthen the bill. Repeat for the second double-dollar strip.

5. Bend the bill strips after the taped creases. Lace one bill into the other bill.

6. Take the far left strip and weave it over the middle strip next to it. Take the far right strip and weave it under the middle strip next to it. Cross the two strips in the center. Push out the weave from the inside using your fingers to shape the outward curve of the ball.

7. Take the far left strip and weave it over the middle strip next to it. Take the far right strip and weave it under the middle strip next to it. Cross the two strips in the center. Push out the weave from the inside using your fingers to shape the outward curve of the ball.

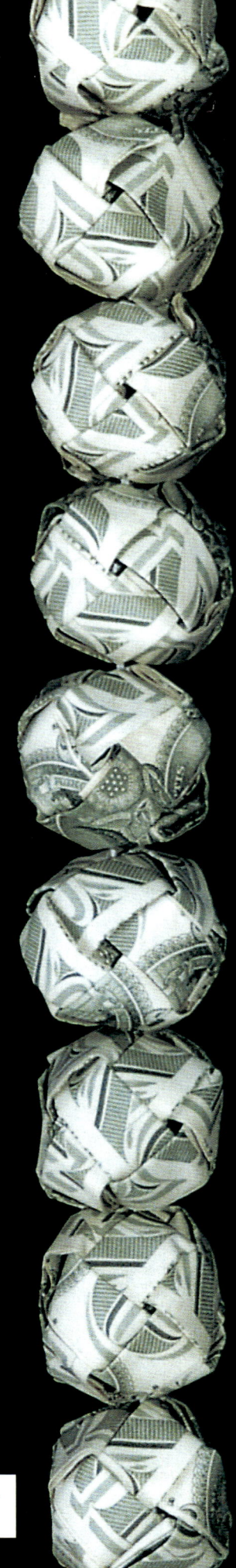

8. Take the far left strip and weave it over the middle strip next to it. Take the far right strip and weave it under the middle strip next to it. Cross the two strips in the center. Push out the weave from the inside using your fingers to shape the outward curve of the ball.

9. Take the far left strip and weave it over the middle strip next to it. Take the far right strip and weave it under the middle strip next to it. Cross the two strips at the center. Push out the weave from the inside using your fingers to shape the outward curve of the ball.

10. Take the far left strip and weave it over the middle strip next to it. Take the far right strip and weave it under the middle strip next to it. Cross the two strips in the center. Push out the weave from the inside using your fingers to shape the outward curve of the ball.

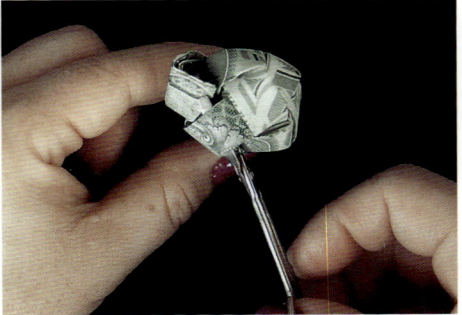

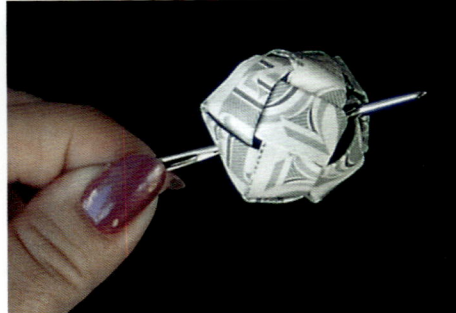

11. Take the far left strip and weave it over the middle strip next to it. Take the far right strip and weave it under the middle strip next to it. Cross the two strips in the center. Push out the weave from the inside using your fingers to shape the outward curve of the ball.

12. Finish the ball by tucking the ends of the bills into the woven ball. Tuck in the ends of the bill following the same woven pattern. Use tweezers to pull the bill through the weave.

13. Cut a piece of lei string 104" in length. Insert the string through the needle. Tie a knot 6" from the open end of the string. Add a toothpick to the end of the string to secure the first ball. Pierce the balls onto the needle without piercing the bills.

14. Pull the balls down to the end of the string. Continue until all balls are strung. Tie a knot to close the lei. Trim off the excess string and remove the toothpick. Add a bow if desired.

Zig-Zag Dollar Lei

One bill makes one link. This is an easy child project. May add decorations. May overlap and tie the ends to join the lei, creating a flat lei.

Makes a 40" lei.

MATERIALS:

72 dollar bills, crisp

1. Fold in half lengthwise to crease. Open the fold.

2. Fold the two sides toward the center.

3. Fold the bill in half lengthwise.

4. Fold the bill in half widthwise.

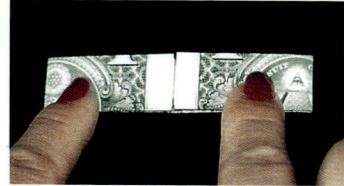

5. Fold the two sides toward the center crease. Repeat steps 1 to 5 for seventy-two bills.

6. Insert a folded bill into the first folded bill.

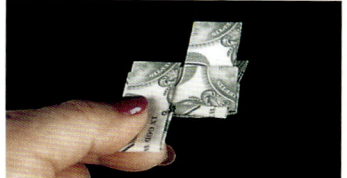

7. Flip the folded bills over. Insert another bill into the last inserted bill. Continue until all bills are joined.

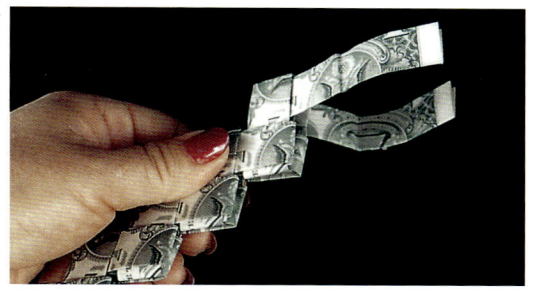

8. Open the two ends of the last attached bill to close the lei.

9. Insert the two ends into the first bill through the two inside openings.

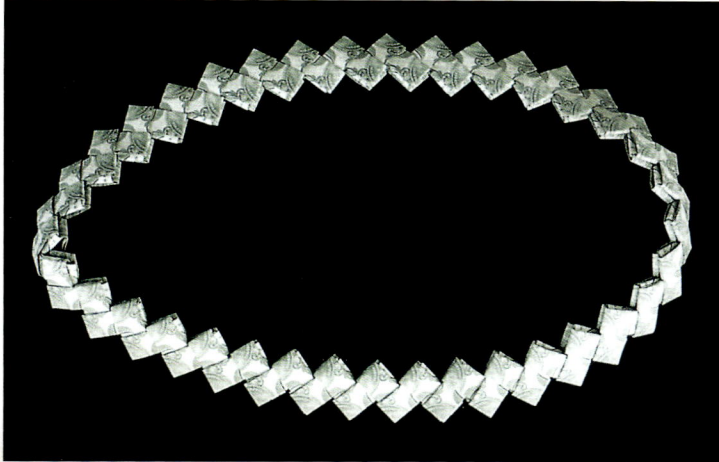

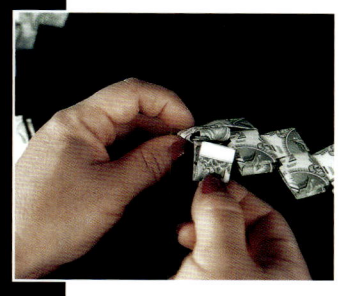

10. Tuck the two end flaps into the first bill to hide and secure the lei connection.

Bibliography

Eng, Norma. *Money Folding Double Your $ 101*. Fort Worth, Texas: Design Originals by Suzanne McNeill, 2002.

Fukumoto, Jodi. *The Guide to Hawaiian-Style Money Folds*. Waipahu, Hawai'i: Island Heritage Publishing, 2002.

Johnson, Ann Akers. *The Buck Book*. Palo Alto, California: Klutz Press, 1993.

Notes

Notes